THE 100 BEST SWIMMING DRILLS

ID0624550

DEDICATION

To the many members of the many venues of the Swimming Technique class, whose ongoing passion for better swimming has inspired me all these years.

THE 100 BEST
SWIMMING DRILLS

Blythe Lucero

Meyer & Meyer Sport

British Library Cataloguing in Publication Data
A catalogue record for this book is available from the British Library

The 100 Best Swimming Drills
Maidenhead: Meyer & Meyer Sport (UK) Ltd., 2008
ISBN 978-1-84126-337-3

All rights reserved, especially the right to copy and distribute,
including the translation rights. No part of this work may be reproduced—
including by photocopy, microfilm or any other means—
processed, stored electronically, copied or distributed in any form whatsoever
without the written permission of the publisher.

© 2008 by Meyer & Meyer Sport (UK) Ltd.
3rd edition 2011
Auckland, Beirut, Budapest, Cairo, Cape Town, Dubai, Indianapolis,
Kindberg, Maidenhead, Sydney, Olten, Singapore, Tehran, Toronto
Member of the World
Sport Publishers' Association (WSPA)
www.w-s-p-a.org
Printed by: B.O.S.S Druck und Medien GmbH, Germany
ISBN 978-1-84126-337-3
E-Mail: info@m-m-sports.com
www.m-m-sports.com

TABLE OF CONTENTS

As long as I have been a swimming coach, I have shied away from the "self help" approach to swimming improvement. The reason is that I believe there is no replacement for an experienced eye observing a swimmer's stroke in action. While a particular stroke may seem right to a swimmer doing it, analysis by a coach can provide valuable insight about subtle, but important stroke flaws that are present. Unchecked, the swimmer can end up practicing and perfecting flawed technique. Without intervention, stroke flaws may be repeated over and over again, becoming habit. This can slow progress, cause frustration with the sport, and, in some instances, eventually lead to injury.

A coach's input is important. By looking beyond what seems to be even a picture perfect stroke, to the heart of swimming efficiency, a coach can identify problem areas and teach the swimmer to avoid poor stroke habits through correct practice. One of the ways coaches encourage correct practice is with swimming drills. Specific drills, targeting specific aspects of the stroke, help the swimmer practice correct technique and relearn ingrained swimming patterns. Once stroke flaws are identified, the swimmer can use stroke drills to address problem areas, and successfully practice on his or her own.

So, the purpose of this book is not to encourage coachless swimming, but to give you tools to work on stroke problems identified by your coach. And while the quest for better swimming is universal, every coach has his or her favorite drills. There are many paths to swimming efficiency. Out of the thousands of swimming drills that have been developed by coaches and swimmers over time, these represent this coach's 100 favorite. Study them. Know their purpose. Try them. Practice them, and practice more. But above all, ask your coach for feedback. There is nothing more valuable than that.

This book has been designed for use in two ways. If you are seeking to improve your swimming efficiency all around, you can start with the first drill and work your way through the book, one stroke at a time. The book is organized into sections by stroke: freestyle, backstroke, breaststroke and butterfly. Within each stroke section, the drills are arranged into subsections addressing body position, kick, arm stroke, breathing, leverage and coordination. Working from start to finish, you can build the technique of one stroke, and then move on to the next.

Or, if you wish to focus on a particular stroke problem, you can turn directly to the section for that stroke. As often, one drill is built upon the skills of the previous drill, it is advisable to read the whole stroke section. After becoming familiar with the basic concepts of the stroke, then focus in on the particular subsection addressing the aspect of technique that you want to work on. Build your technique one drill at a time. Finally, turn to the subsection on coordination, and use these drills to reintegrate your stroke with your new technique.

Whichever approach you choose, it is important to study the purpose of each drill, and to keep that purpose in mind while practicing. Follow the steps and refer to the diagrams and photos to perform the drill correctly. Don't get discouraged if things don't fall into place right away. Drills are meant to be repeated, and repeated again. Check the Drill Feedback Charts to identify problems. Make modifications and try again. Practice over several visits to the pool. Above all, spend lots of time in the water, and enjoy every minute of it.

IN PURSUIT OF EFFICIENT SWIMMING

THE ART AND THE SCIENCE OF SWIMMING

The process of becoming an efficient swimmer involves using both the body and the brain to "feel" and "understand" what is going on. When a swimmer "feels" fluid movement through the water, and "understands" the cause and effect of specific actions, that swimmer is prepared to pursue efficient swimming.

The art of swimming is all about "feeling" effective movement through the water. It is probably best described as "being at one with the water". A good example of the art of swimming is when good swimmers refer to feeling fishlike in the water. The movement achieved by efficient swimmers is fluid, like the strokes of an artist's brush. It is also graceful, as a swimmer uses balance, rhythm and posture, much like the art of dance. And, it is powerful, like musical harmony, as the combined actions of the swimmer's body produce a greater result to each action alone. The art of swimming means a swimmer is able to "feel" the water, rather than fight it.

The science of swimming is all about "understanding" movement through the water. There is a lot of physics at work in swimming. By understanding these principles, a swimmer can learn to apply them to the water. Coach Doc Counsilman, revered as "the father of modern swimming" described the ingredients in successful swimming as "water, brains and guts." Using the science of swimming, a swimmer can study movement through the water as an equation, and can begin to figure it out. The science of swimming means a swimmer is able to "understand" how to produce the most propulsion with the least effort.

Because good swimming is a matter of feeling and understanding, the most beneficial practice engages both body and brain.

13

Swimming drills are examples of this kind of practice. Drills are extremely useful tools because they encourage the swimmer to approach swimming as both an art and a science.

THE TECHNIQUE OF ECONOMIC SWIMMING

The first step in becoming an efficient swimmer, is becoming an economic swimmer. The distinction between these two stages is subtle, but very important to understand in working through the progression of swimming development. Economic swimming refers to managing the energy resources required for the effort of swimming. Swimming efficiency refers to the quality and quantity produced through that effort.

How a swimmer manages his or her energy makes a big difference in how much effort can be put forth to swim faster for longer. Swimming that requires more effort uses more energy that is depleted more quickly. The amount of energy a swimmer has available, like gas in the tank of a car, is not unlimited. The effort it takes to move through the water is one of the primary variables that makes one swimmer faster than another swimmer. Through ongoing attention to the mechanics of swimming, a swimmer can learn to move through the water with less effort, and become an economic swimmer.

The foundation of economic swimming is solid swimming technique that allows a swimmer to minimize drag, to develop "feel" for the water, and to access potential power. By learning to minimize drag, swimmers can make prudent use of their effort, and save energy. By learning to feel the water, swimmers can be thrifty with their energy, avoiding the wasted effort of extra strokes. By learning to access potential power, swimmers can expend less energy, by engaging the muscle groups best suited to move the body forward with the least effort.

One of the best ways to make the connection between swimming technique and economic swimming is through swimming drills. Drills

for swimming technique are useful tools in feeling and understanding economic swimming. Swimming drills teach economic swimming by focusing on the mechanics that allow a swimmer to move through the water with less drag, better feeling for the water, and more access to potential power.

TURNING WORKOUT INTO PRACTICE

Efficient swimming is achieved when the valuable energy conserved through the technique of economic swimming, can be applied to sustaining speed over time in the water. The bridge from economic to efficient swimming should be formed in two ways. First, a swimmer should devote time in the water to ongoing practice of economic swimming based on good technique. This includes active work on positive floatation, productive kicking, aligned and accelerating arm stroke, balanced recovery, rhythmic breathing, and effective use of core leverage. Simultaneously, a swimmer should dedicate time to developing the conditioning and strength necessary to apply that solid swimming, stroke after stroke. This includes increasing cardiovascular endurance, well-rounded fitness, and muscle tone, as well as building fast twitch muscle fiber, and an increased threshold for the repetitive action of swimming.

Too often, concern with stroke technique is left behind soon after a swimmer is able to produce forward motion, and time and attention are devoted to conditioning only. This one-sided approach is reinforced as the swimmer is rewarded by rapid improvement, often for quite a while. However, there comes a point when improvement through conditioning alone stops, because working out is only half the formula to improved swimming.

Regular attention to technique increases a swimmer's capacity for improvement, by developing swimming that requires less effort. The swimmer is then able to apply energy saved to building better swimming through efficient strokes. By focusing on solid stroke mechanics during every swimming session, a swimmer can transform a workout from an opportunity to swim more, into an opportunity to practice efficient swimming.

Swimming drills are excellent tools to focus a swimmer's efforts toward swimming efficiency. They can be strategically incorporated into any swim session. A routine that includes specific practice, like drills, rather than just workout, allows a swimmer to experience long term swimming improvement by building efficient swimming from the technique side and the conditioning side simultaneously.

WHAT DRILLS ARE ALL ABOUT

WHAT IS A DRILL?

A drill is a structured method of practice used to acquire a skill, procedure or sequence. We use drills to acquire a vast array of everyday and specialized skills. We use drills to learn everything from cursive writing to tying our shoes, from cheer leading formations to military exercises. Drills are designed to make a particular skill, sequence or procedure easier to absorb, retain and recall. They combine a thinking and feeling approach to learning, so skills can be developed, practiced and performed better.

Drills are widely used by athletes to master and excel at physically demanding skills that require precise technique, and quick, continuous application. In swimming, a drill can be defined as:

- An activity designed to develop and practice good stroke habits
- A repetitive exercise for improving and perfecting stroke technique
- A way of isolating part of a complex stroke sequence, to learn and perform it correctly

Swimming drills address various aspects of the stroke, including:

BODY POSITION

As human beings, we are comfortable and agile moving about on land. We have mastered vertical balance. To be a good swimmer, we must become equally comfortable and agile in the water. We have to master horizontal balance, or floating. Just as we are able to shift

our weight forward and from side to side to do things better and easier on land, we must learn this skill in the water. Learning to float well is an essential skill for swimming efficiently. Our spine and core strength are key in allowing us to stand erectly, and they are equally crucial in floating correctly. Swimmers are well served by giving special attention to learning how to stabilize their core in the water. Developing this skill allows the swimmer to be in control of how he or she floats. It reduces drag, improves feel for the water, and increases access to power. It encourages the swimmer to achieve the important feeling of swimming "downhill".

KICK

The role of the legs in swimming is to provide forward momentum, rhythm, and counterbalance to other actions of the stroke. While the large muscles of the legs are an invaluable resource to swimmers, they demand a great deal of oxygen. It is therefore worthwhile to develop good kicking skills. Swimmers should strive to develop both a productive and a sustainable kick. A productive kick can relieve the upper body of some of the workload. A sustainable kick is economical in terms of energy expenditure. Although a consequence of kicking is that the legs will float better, this should not be the primary focus of kicking. Kicking should be used for forward motion, not to correct floating problems. Kicking well requires a swimmer to have relaxed feet and ankles, fluid motion, and above all to keep the feet connected to the water.

ARM STROKE

The power phase of the arm stroke, or what the arms do underwater to move us forward must be worked on in three dimensions: length, width and depth. Although the path of the arms is unique to each stroke, the arms have three basic functions in all strokes. The arms are the primary tools we use to maximize the length of our stroke. Longer strokes mean fewer strokes. Fewer strokes mean less energy to cover a certain distance. The arms are also used to move the body forward, in the straightest, most direct path to our destination.

Using sculling or sweeping motions, the arm action increases speed as it travels through the stroke, causing the body to advance. Most importantly of all, the arms are used to position our hands so we can best feel the water. Hands that are able to feel the water are able use the water like a handle. With a firm hold on the water, the swimmer can best move his or her body forward past the point at which the hands are anchored.

RECOVERY

The recovery follows the underwater arm stroke, returning the arm to its starting point in front for another stroke. In all strokes except breaststroke, recovery is the phase when the swimmer's arms can rest momentarily. Learning to relax during recovery is an important skill to develop in working towards the most economical swimming style. Alignment of the recovery is often overlooked as a factor in swimming efficiency. A misaligned recovery can lead to a misaligned arm stroke, requiring constant correcting to be done, at the expense of forward motion. An aligned recovery is also an excellent preventive measure in remaining pain and injury free in the vulnerable shoulder area. Lastly, a relaxed and aligned recovery works to balance the rest of the stroke. Even though the recovery does not itself move a swimmer forward, it is by nature connected to the other actions of the stroke. It is important to recover in a way that complements and perpetuates the forward motion of the stroke.

BREATHING

Replenishing the body with oxygen is an integral part of any sport, but in swimming, the added challenge of doing so while in the water makes breathing a primary aspect of swimming technique. Swimmers must learn to breathe rhymically to best fuel their bodies. In addition, they must learn to inhale and exhale within the line of the stroke to avoid disrupting the forward motion of their swimming. In general, timing the inhale with the stroke's recovery, and timing the exhale to the power phase makes breathing fit into the forward motion best, without creating insurmountable drag. This timing also

places the exhale to the part of the stroke that demands the most exertion. So as in other sports, and in life in general, the swimmer can summon more power by expelling air while applying force. Some scholars of swimming believe that the rhythm of swimming should actually be determined by a swimmer's natural breathing rhythm. This theory makes breathing the central focus in developing the most effective stroke rate, pace, and strategy. Whether you are sprinting a 50 or swimming a mile, breathing technique is a factor in your ability to swim better.

LEVERAGE

Although we use our limbs to press against the water, the power to use them comes from our core. Like a ceiling fan, with its blades turning, what is propelling the movement is the motor in the middle, or in the case of the swimmer, the core. This core-centered power is visible in many forms of athletics. Observe a baseball pitcher preparing to throw the ball. It is the pitcher's arm throwing the ball, yet look at the pitcher's hips and shoulders turn to the side in preparation. As the ball leaves the hand, the same side hip and shoulder snap forward. It is actually the core that is powering that pitch. You can observe this same core leverage in action with the batter as well. You can see it in a golfer, a boxer, and an ice skater, among others.

Leverage is also present in the limbs while swimming. To access available leverage, swimmers must learn to stabilize their joints, especially the elbows and the knees. Observe fish. They don't have elbows or knees. If our goal is to swim as efficiently as fish, we have to learn to stabilize our joints, and not allow them to collapse and weaken our levers.

COORDINATION

The numerous actions that make up swimming are each pieces in a puzzle, that when fitted correctly together, create fluid, graceful and powerful forward motion. Each action has its purpose, and its

relationship to the whole. While it is important to develop each action in itself, connecting them together so they work in harmony is what efficient swimming is all about. We must learn to use our kick with our arms, not just in addition to our arms. We must learn to breathe within the line of the stroke, so the necessary act of breathing does not interrupt our forward motion. We must learn to deliberately use good body position to access leverage, which affects the arm stroke, recovery, breathing and kick.

Swimming efficiently is a matter of coordinated action. We must learn to time each action so that it complements the other elements of the stroke, rather than working against them. We must strive to develop our weakest actions, and make the most of our strongest ones. All of this must be done with one goal in mind: to move through the water with less effort so it can be done faster and longer.

TYPES OF SWIMMING DRILLS

Swimming is a complex sequence of actions. Like driving, playing guitar, or typing, multiple crucial actions are performed at once, or in tight succession. Correct technique is necessary or the result is unsatisfactory. Certain types of drills are very successful for developing skills that are complex in nature, like swimming. These include:

PROGRESSION BASED DRILLS

Swimming drills based in "progression" allow the swimmer to build a stroke, one piece at a time. Beginning with a basic skill, the swimmer can concentrate on developing the stroke in steps, from simple to complex. Once the first action is mastered, the swimmer can add on another part. Eventually, all the parts of the stroke are connected, and the swimmer can then feel and understand them in the context of the coordinated stroke.

PART PRACTICE

When a stroke flaw is identified, new stroke habits can be established with "part practice" drills. Part practice encourages positive change by isolating a particular action of the stroke, and providing repetitive practice of just that part of the stroke. By narrowing the focus, the swimmer is able to relearn a weak part of their stroke, and implement the new correct technique upon resuming the full stroke.

CONTRAST DRILLS

To underscore the correct way of doing a skill, "contrast drills" start by having the swimmer perform the skill incorrectly. The skill is then immediately repeated, with specific changes, which correct the technique. By contrasting the right and the wrong way of performing a skill, the swimmer is guided to choose the better technique by noticing better results from using the correct technique. Using negative examples is a controversial practice, however, when followed up with correct practice, can be an effective learning tool.

X DRILLS

In order to emphasize a particular point of technique, "X drills" use eXaggeration to demonstrate the effect of a particular stroke action. By taking a skill to the eXtreme, a swimmer can more clearly feel the desired technique. When the swimmer is able to eXperience the full effect of a particular technique, its purpose is more obvious. X drills allow the swimmer to eXplore the full range of a stroke action and to discover how to best balance various stroke actions with each other.

HISTORY OF SWIMMING DRILLS

Swimming has been a part of the human experience throughout history. Little is known about the methods used by early civilizations to acquire swimming skills, but swimming is depicted in Egyptian

and Assyrian art dating back to 2000 B.C. Probably originally learned for survival, artifacts show that swimming was used for military purposes as well as leisure in ancient times. It is mentioned in the Bible, and was considered an important part of education by the Romans. Swimming was called the highest sport by the prophet Mohammed. It was also one of the original "agilities" needed to become a knight.

The first books addressing the technique of swimming were published beginning in the 1500s. Reflecting the European view of swimming as an activity of culture and sophistication, the technique described resembled the breaststroke. The first swimming drills were presented as diagrams for study and emulation. Later, land practice became a popular method of teaching swimming skills. Learners practiced the swimming actions by moving the arms and legs through the air in a repetitive, disciplined manner. However, this land drill method failed to address floatation, an essential aspect of swimming. Without experience in the water, learners often met with serious consequences! By the 1700s, a drastically different swimming technique was recorded by explorers of the New World, who were fascinated by the alternating over arm stroke they saw among the natives. Although described as superior in speed to their own style, the new swimming technique was not adopted by the Europeans for some time, as their view of good technique centered on graceful swimming, not fast swimming.

When swimming became an official sport in the early 1800s, the goal of swimming became speed. Swimmers experimented with new techniques, and trial and error led to the development of new strokes, including the side stroke, trudgen, and finally the crawl stroke. By the beginning of the 20th century, early swimming coaches were known as professors of swimming claimed to hold the secrets to winning techniques. Beginning in the 1920s, coaches filmed the best swimmers, and used the moving pictures as training tools. By the 1950s, four distinct competitive strokes had been established, with rules defining the acceptable technique for each. Coaches focused on developing speed by having their swimmers do repeat drills, or interval training.

In the 1960s, Coach Doc Counsilman revolutionized the approach to developing swimming speed by addressing swimming efficiency. Using established science to explain swimming propulsion, Counsilman's work focused on the technique of efficient swimming. In an effort to teach this kind of swimming, Counsilman contributed concepts still practiced today, including sculling, and leverage. Over the past forty years, the training methods for competitive swimming have developed rapidly, but practicing good technique with swimming drills has remained a part of training programs at all levels of the sport. Alexander Popov, the "Russian Rocket" promoted freestyle with the dolphin kick. Inge deBraun's coach had her spend hours doing single leg kicking. Natalie Couglin rose to world class status training with no arm work. USA Swimming endorses technique development from the earliest levels of the competitive swimming with the slogan "a skill done 99 % correctly is 100 % wrong". Swimming drills of one kind or another have been used throughout history and they continue to be an effective part of the development of swimmers from novice to world class.

USING SWIMMING DRILLS

WHEN TO USE DRILLS

Because swimming drills are one of a swimmer's best tools for practicing toward efficient swimming, they should be included in every swim session. They can be done as a part of warm-up to establish a foundation for the rest of the practice. They can be used within a set to remind the swimmer of the correct technique as they are working hard and might otherwise sacrifice quality for quantity. They can be used between sets to refocus the swimmer on the goal of swimming efficiently.

Swimming drills are also an excellent part of preparation for competition. As a part of taper, swimming drills provide the swimmer with quality swimming that is less intensive, so the swimmer can maintain a feel for the water while achieving overall recovery from training workload. On race day, drills are excellent as a part of warm-up, allowing the swimmer to practice ideal stroke actions as he or she focuses on the race to come.

During the off-season, a swimmer can use swimming drills almost exclusively to maintain conditioning and practice stroke economy and improve efficiency for the next season.

HOW TO USE DRILLS

When practicing any swimming drill, it is very important to know the purpose of the drill. Just performing a drill is not enough. Doing a drill without understanding its purpose is empty swimming. Without understanding what the desired outcome of the drill is, a swimmer cannot get the full benefit out of practicing it. To be fully engaged, a swimmer must think about and feel both what is supposed to happen, and, what is happening in the drill.

As certain drills are designed to focus a swimmer's practice on a very specific part of the stroke, it is important to concentrate on that particular point, and ignore the rest. For example, a certain drill for kicking may require the arms to be at the sides. This can make breathing difficult, and not at all like the breathing technique used in the complete stroke. But, in this drill, it is important to remember that breathing is not the point. Focusing on the breathing, rather than the kicking, defeats the purpose of the drill.

Likewise, a swimmer must know the correct sequence of the drill, and perform each step correctly. This is important to feel the full effect of the action being performed in the drill. Skipping a step reinforces incorrect technique, and can interfere with achieving the desired outcome. Sometimes, the skipped step is the very one that represents the problem area. Start by practicing each drill slowly. Many drills seem awkward at first, but like any new thing, they get better with practice. Spend time on each drill. Identify problems and make the needed modifications to do the drill right.

There are drills that are designed to be done at swim speed, and drills that are not. Some drills are done in a stationary position. Remember, your concern should not be with the amount of yardage you do, but the quality of what you are doing. Once you are able to do the drill correctly, it can be helpful to alternate laps of drill and swim so the new technique can work in the context of the full stroke.

Remember, there is no rush. By using drills to practice the technique of swimming, you become fully engaged in the process of reaching for swimming efficiency. The achievement of efficient swimming is an excellent goal, but the process toward that goal can be equally rewarding. Each positive change becomes a revelation. Each new skill learned becomes like a piece in a puzzle, discovered unexpectedly after a long search. Every improvement empowers you to pursue another.

THE BEST 100
SWIMMING DRILLS

DRILLS FOR
FREESTYLE

BODY POSITION DRILLS

An efficient freestyle is built on good body position. The way we float in the water is affected by our core tension. For a better freestyle, we must learn to shift weight forward, and achieve a "downhill" floating position. The goal of the following drills for body position is to experience an advantageous float and effective core stability.

Downhill Float

THE PURPOSE OF THIS DRILL
- Learning to shift weight to achieve a "downhill" floating position
- Understanding the importance of a correct head position
- Feeling effective core tension and stability

HOW TO DO THIS DRILL
Step 1: Float face down in the water, with your arms at your sides, in a head leading position. Don't attempt any forward motion.

Step 2: Notice your body position. For most people, the legs will soon begin to sink, leaving the swimmer in an "uphill" floating position.

Step 3: To begin correcting this disadvantageous floating position, lower your chin, so you are looking at the bottom of the pool, not forward. For many people, this simple action will have a positive effect on their float, including raising their sinking legs a bit.

Step 4: Now focus on your spine. Make it as straight as possible by contracting your abdominal muscles and pulling your bellybutton in. Learning to achieve and maintain a straight spine through core tension is an important skill that can be applied to all strokes.

Step 5: While holding your core stable, lean forward on your chest. Doing so should allow your hips and legs to rise toward the surface of the water. This is the desirable "downhill" floating position upon which you can build a good freestyle.

Step 6: Stand, breathe and again lay horizontally in the water, face down, this time with your arms extended over your head, hands leading. Look at the bottom of the pool, achieve a straight spine and stable core. Shift your weight forward and feel the "downhill" float.

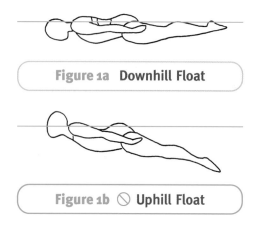

Figure 1a **Downhill Float**

Figure 1b ⊘ **Uphill Float**

DRILL FEEDBACK CHART

Problem	Modification
My legs still sink.	For some people, either because of densely muscular legs, or low body fat, their legs will tend to sink no matter what. For these people it is all the more important to learn to hold their core in a "downhill" floating position.
I can't balance on my chest.	Try rotating your shoulders back, and rounding your chest out. Pretend you are standing at attention horizontally. Focus on your breastbone, moving it gently lower in the water.
I can't breathe.	This drill requires you to hold your breath. When you run out of air, simply stand up and start again.

Log Roll

2

THE PURPOSE OF THIS DRILL
- Maintaining the horizontal axis while rolling
- Accessing power from your core
- Getting comfortable floating "downhill" in a non-flat position

HOW TO DO THIS DRILL
Step 1: Float face down in the water, arms at your sides, head leading, without attempting any forward motion. Achieve a "downhill" float and position your head so you are looking at the bottom of the pool.

Step 2: Maintaining your core tension and head position, roll onto your right side by rotating your right hip and shoulder one quarter turn clockwise. Hold for 5 seconds.

Step 3: Maintaining your core tension and head position, roll onto your back by rotating your right hip and shoulder one quarter turn clockwise. Hold for 5 seconds.

Step 4: Maintaining your core tension and head position, roll onto your left side by rotating your right hip and shoulder one quarter turn clockwise. Hold for 5 seconds.

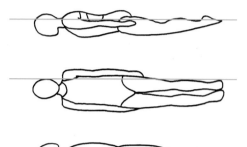

Step 5: Maintaining your core tension and head position, roll back onto your front by rotating your right hip and shoulder one quarter turn clockwise. Hold for 5 seconds.

Step 6: Stand, breathe, then repeat this drill rolling counter clockwise.

Figure 2 Log Roll

DRILL FEEDBACK CHART

Problem	Modification
I can't get a quarter turn.	Try initiating the turn from the hip and letting your shoulder follow.
My sinking legs get in the way.	You can do this drill with a very light kick if necessary.
I can't breathe.	You can catch a breath when you rotate to your back.

Twelve Kick Switch Freestyle

3

THE PURPOSE OF THIS DRILL
- Maintaining a "downhill" float while moving
- Beginning to feel leverage from the core
- Identifying the longest freestyle position

HOW TO DO THIS DRILL

Step 1: Float on your side in the water, arm towards the surface at your side, the arm closest to the bottom of the pool extended over your head. Engage core tension to achieve the "downhill" float.

Step 2: Begin a gentle but continuous flutter kick, which should also be directed side to side, rather than up and down.

Step 3: If you are properly aligned, your face will be mostly submerged. To breathe, maintain a stable head position and roll towards your back, breathe, then roll back to your original side position. Create a regular breathing interval.

Step 4: Kick twelve times (each leg equals one kick).

Step 5: Just as you finish the last kick, bring the side laying arm over the water to the front, and the forward reaching arm through the water to your side. At the same time, switch to the opposite side of your body to float.

Step 6: Do twelve more kicks in this position. Repeat the switch with your arms and floating side. Continue to kick twelve times then switch to the far end of the pool.

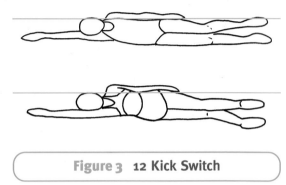

Figure 3   **12 Kick Switch**

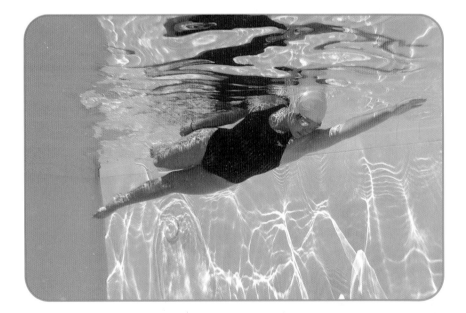

DRILL FEEDBACK CHART

Problem	Modification
I go crooked.	Try to align your body and reaching arm.
My kick is not side to side.	This is usually a result of your hips not being aligned to the side with your shoulders. Use more core tension.
I can't maintain a "downhill" float.	Check your head position. During the twelve kicks, your lower ear should be resting on the shoulder of your reaching arm.

KICK DRILLS

A productive flutter kick is part of a good freestyle. It provides constant momentum, and counterbalance to the arm stroke. Because the legs require a disproportionate amount of energy, developing a relaxed, sustainable kick is important. The goal of the following freestyle kicking drills is to learn to use an economical flutter kick that will enhance the rest of the freestyle stroke.

Toe Point Drill

THE PURPOSE OF THIS DRILL
- Understanding the importance of a pointed toe kick
- Experimenting with foot pitch
- Develop a centralized kick

HOW TO DO THIS DRILL
Step 1: Lay horizontally in the water, face down, arms extended. To breathe, do a simple press outward on the water with your hands, and

35

raise your chin gently to the surface, then to return your face to the water, and bring your hands back together in an extended position.

Step 2: Begin doing the flutter kick, using alternating up and down motion with your leg. Kick to a depth of about twelve to fifteen inches, and up to the surface of the water. Kick briskly with relaxed, but fairly straight legs.

Step 3: Focus on your foot position. To best engage the water, you must use the largest surface of your feet to push against the water. Position your feet so your toes are pointed. Kick briskly for 30 seconds. Feel the tops and the bottoms of your feet push the water as your feet sweep up and down.

Step 4: Now, flex your feet at the ankles, setting them at right angles to your leg (the standing foot position). Kick briskly for 30 seconds. Feel the smaller surface with which you are pushing the water. Notice that you don't move forward well. Some people can even move backwards with this foot position!

Step 5: Now, reposition your feet so your toes are pointed, and rotate your knees and feet inward, so that your toes are closer together than your heels. Together, your feet should form a point. Kick briskly for 30 seconds. Feel a larger foot surface pressing against the water. Notice that your kick is much more effective, with much less effort, and that there is one centralized splash at your feet.

Figure 4a **Toes Pointed**

Step 6: Continue kicking with your toes pointed and your feet rotated inward. Kick briskly, with relaxed feet. Feel your kick move you forward as you sweep the water down with the tops of your feet, and up with the bottoms of your feet. Kick to the far end of the pool.

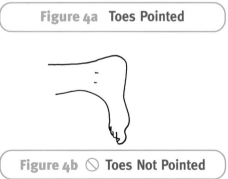

Figure 4b ⊘ **Toes Not Pointed**

DRILL FEEDBACK CHART

Problem	Modification
My kick makes a huge splash, no matter what foot position I use.	Splash from your kick should be a result of your foot moving water, rather than your foot bringing air down into the water. Bend your knees less. Keep your feet connected to the water.
When I turn my feet inward, my big toes bump into each other.	You are fortunate to have excellent foot pitch! As you practice the drill more, adjust your knee rotation a bit to avoid your toes bumping, but do so as little as possible.
I get cramps in the arches of my feet when I point my toes.	Try pointing your foot and letting your toes be relaxed. As humans, this position is not natural for us. It can be improved as you practice more.

Floppy Foot Drill

THE PURPOSE OF THIS DRILL
- Developing a relaxed kick
- Experiencing fish-like propulsion
- Learning to conserve energy

HOW TO DO THIS DRILL

Step 1: Observe a fish swimming. Any fish will do: your pet gold fish, or a shark at the aquarium. Notice the tail as the fish swims. It is not rigid, rather it moves back and forth in the water like a flag in the breeze. It is fluid. The movement is not frantic, rather, it appears to be an effortless action for the fish.

Step 2: Put on a single, long swim fin on one foot and stand in the water, and stand in the water with your back against the wall, submerging the entire fin under the water. Sweep your leg up and down in the water covering about twenty four inches of distance each way. Use enough speed so you feel the resistance of the fin against the water. Notice how the water bends the fin as it moves. Notice how when your leg sweeps in the one direction, the fin bends the opposite way. The movement is fluid, like the tail of the fish.

Step 3: Now, take off the fin and float face down in the water, arms extended. Begin kicking briskly, keeping your feet connected to the water, moving within about fifteen inches of depth. Point your toes, but relax your feet so the water bends them like it did the fin. Kick briskly for 30 seconds. Think about the effortless and fluid motion of the fish tail. Let the water move your foot as if it was a flag in the wind. Rest, then practice again.

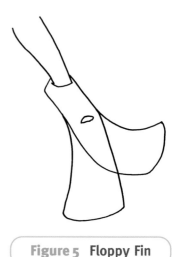

Step 4: Once you develop a fluid, floppy foot kick, notice that the splash

Figure 5 Floppy Fin

from your kick is much more compact, and your kick is more productive. Practice for several lengths of the pool.

DRILL FEEDBACK CHART

Problem	Modification
My feet are stiff.	Try achieving the feeling on land to start. First try it with your hand. Relax your wrist and flop your hand back and forth. Now stand on one leg and relax your other ankle. Shake your other foot until it flops like your hand did. Next, sweep your leg forward, as if kicking a ball, foot relaxed. Watch your foot. By the farthest extent of the movement, your relaxed foot should flop forward. Now try it in the water.
I don't feel resistance on my feet.	Kick more briskly. Try changing the depth of your kick. It should pass through about fifteen inches of water. Relax your ankles.
I get tired too quickly to notice a floppy kicking motion.	Give it time. Remember using the large muscles of your legs to initiate the kick will initially use more oxygen than a less effective kick, thus making you feel tired and out of breath. The muscles adapt relatively quickly as you practice.

6 Vertical Kicking Sequence

THE PURPOSE OF THIS DRILL
- Understanding the importance of foot speed
- Engaging the correct muscles for flutter kick
- Feeling the water with your feet

HOW TO DO THIS DRILL
Step 1: In water at least as deep as you are tall, get into a vertical position. Engage your core. Begin a gentle sculling action (tracing side to side underwater figure eights with your hands) to keep your head above water.

Step 2: Without producing forward or backwards motion, begin kicking the flutter kick, moving your extended legs in a sweeping motion alternately so that when one foot is forward, the other is back, within a range of approximately twelve to fifteen inches. Your toes should be pointed towards the bottom of the pool, and your feet and knees should be rotated slightly inward.

Step 3: Focus on the muscles you are engaging. They should be the large muscles, high in your legs. As you move your leg forward, you should be feeling your quadriceps. As you move your leg back, you should feel your hamstrings and glutes working.

Step 4: Your legs should be fairly straight, yet not locked at the knee as you kick. As you increase the speed of your kick, forward and backward, avoid raising your knees as if marching or bicycling. It should feel like your legs are sweeping back and forth, like a broom through the water.

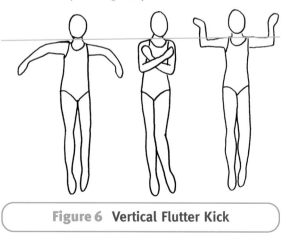

Figure 6 Vertical Flutter Kick

Step 5: Kick even faster. Try to achieve a fluid motion that makes your legs feel as if they have no bones. Try to maintain your head up while kicking for 30 seconds.

Step 6: Once you have achieved a fluid, comfortable kick, it is time to check its effectiveness by stopping the sculling action with your hands. Cross your hands over your chest positioning your left hand on the right shoulder, and your right hand on your left shoulder. Kick, keeping your head above water. Maintain for 30 seconds.

Step 7: When you are able to keep your head up without the help of arm movements, try the advanced version of this drill: position your arms so they extend side to side at the surface of the water. Now raise your hands out of the water, bending at a right angle at the elbow. Kick! Can you keep your head up for 30 seconds?

DRILL FEEDBACK CHART

Problem	Modification
I sink even when I am sculling.	Use straighter legs. Point your toes. Kick faster.
I bounce up and down.	Use a narrower, quicker kicking motion, rather than a scissor type kick.
I feel the kick in my calves.	Relax your feet more. Use less knee bend. Try to initiate the kick from higher on your leg, where the muscles are larger and stronger.

7 Single Leg Kicking

THE PURPOSE OF THIS DRILL
- Developing an effective, full leg kick
- Feeling a continuous kick
- Keeping the foot connected to the water

HOW TO DO THIS DRILL
Step 1: Position a kick-board under your arms, hands at the far end, to support your upper body and keep your face out of the water. Hold the kick-board flat on the water.

Step 2: Begin kicking the flutter kick with your right leg only. Allow your left leg to simply float. Kick briskly for 30 seconds. Rest.

Step 3: Try again. Use your whole leg to kick, not just from the knee down. Notice that as you begin to perfect this skill, your kicking leg is moving very quickly, with no pause at the top or the bottom of the kick. Notice too, that you are pushing water in both directions: up and down.

Step 4: Rest, then try it with the other leg for 30 seconds. Notice that if you allow your foot to come out of the water at the top of the kick, it is less effective than when it stays connected to the water.

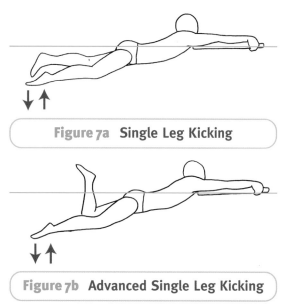

Figure 7a   Single Leg Kicking

Figure 7b   Advanced Single Leg Kicking

Step 5: Once you are able to create forward motion with one leg, try the advanced version of this drill.

Bend your left leg at the knee, raise your heel, and hold it out of the water at a right angle. Kick very briskly with your right leg, with no pause at the top or the bottom of the motion. Use your whole leg to sweep the water. Kick for 30 seconds. Switch legs and kick for another 30 seconds.

Step 6: After you rest, then kick regular flutter kicks with both legs, trying to simulate the same kicking you just finished with a single leg. Use your whole leg to kick to the same depth and same height. Use the same muscles and the same kick rate. Use the same continuous motion only this time alternate legs with each kick.

DRILL FEEDBACK CHART

Problem	Modification
I seem to go uphill with the kickboard.	Press down on the kick-board with your arms and chest. Hold it parallel to the surface of the water.
I don't move.	Try kicking with a bit more force, not necessarily a larger kick, just stronger. Don't stop the kick at the top or the bottom.
I am making a lot of splash.	Use less knee bend. Move the water both up and down. Keep your feet connected to the water.

ARM STROKE DRILLS

With the long, sweeping, alternating arm action of the freestyle stroke, humans are capable of producing the most potential speed of all the strokes. To develop an efficient freestyle, the swimmer must be concerned with three things. First, achieving correct alignment is crucial to begin the stroke from a position of strength. Second, maintaining a high elbow position is important to hold on to the water. Third, accelerating through the arm stroke is necessary to fully benefit from the stroke action. The goal of the following arm stroke drills for freestyle is to develop a productive arm stroke, to make the most of the power phase of the stroke.

Pull/Push Freestyle

THE PURPOSE OF THIS DRILL
- Feeling the path of the freestyle arm stroke
- Achieving a high elbow position
- Using the full length of the stroke

HOW TO DO THIS DRILL
Step 1: Push off the wall, face down, arms extended, core engaged, looking at the bottom of the pool. Establish a continuous flutter kick.

Step 2: Do a freestyle arm stroke with your right arm. Start by pitching your fingertips and the palm of your hand down slightly, adjusting them to press back on the water, instead of pressing down. Allow your forearm to follow, but keep your elbow high and firm. Sweep your hand slightly outward and down, then inward until it lines up under your shoulder. At this point, your elbow should be in line with your hand and shoulder, but sticking out as if you were trying to nudge someone. This is the "pull" portion of the freestyle arm stroke.

Step 3: From there, press back quickly on the water with your hand. Feel your hand pass your elbow. Adjust the pitch of your hand to maintain pressure back on the water. Sweep your hand back until your arm is straight. Your hand should pass your hip and finish with your thumb touching your thigh. This is the "push" portion of the freestyle arm stroke.

Step 4: Return your hand over the water to the front reaching position. When it passes your shoulder, begin the arm stroke with your left arm, pitching your fingertips and hands downward and allowing your forearm to follow. Press back on the water until your hand lines up under your shoulder, with your elbow pointed out to the side. Then press back quickly past your elbow until your arm is straight, past your hip. Notice that as your stroke goes from pull to push, it also goes from deeper to shallower.

Step 5: Bring your arm left back to the front over the water, starting the next stroke with your right arm when the left arm passes your shoulder out of the water. Continue stroking. Use the full length of each arm stroke. Maintain a

45

high elbow position. Feel the pull and the push of each stroke. Practice for several lengths of the pool until you can clearly distinguish the pull and the push motions of the freestyle stroke.

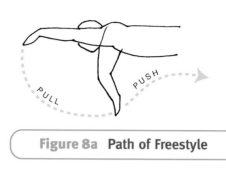

Figure 8a Path of Freestyle

Figure 8c 🚫 Low Elbow Position

Figure 8b High Elbow Position

DRILL FEEDBACK CHART

Problem	Modification
I don't feel the "pull".	Keep your elbow still while you start the stroke with your hand. Pitch your fingertips and palm downward. Press back on the water, not down.
I don't feel the "push".	Keep your elbow high and firm. Allow your hand to push past it. If your elbow drops back, you won't be able to accomplish the push well. Accelerate the motion toward your hip.
I can't do many strokes because I have to stop and breathe.	Take a big breath and do four to six long strokes, then stand, breathe, and start again.

Catch Up

9

THE PURPOSE OF THIS DRILL
- Practicing a long stroke
- Feeling acceleration in the arm stroke
- Developing a high elbow underwater arm stroke

HOW TO DO THIS DRILL

Step 1: Push off the wall, face down, arms extended, core engaged, looking at the bottom of the pool. Your arms should be aligned in front of your shoulders, not in front of your nose. Establish a continuous flutter kick, which should be maintained throughout the drill.

Step 2: With your right arm still extended and aligned with the shoulder, perform a single freestyle arm stroke with your left arm. With your fingertips and palm pitched down slightly, press back on the water, not down. Keep your elbow high and firm as your forearm follows your hand. Pull then push, sweeping your hand from deep to shallow toward your hip, accelerating the motion from front to back, until your arm is straight at your side.

Step 3: From this position, your right arm extended in front of you, and left arm at your side, feel the full length of your stroke. Return the left arm over the water to the starting point, so both arms are again at full extension. Then, perform a single stroke with your right in the same manner.

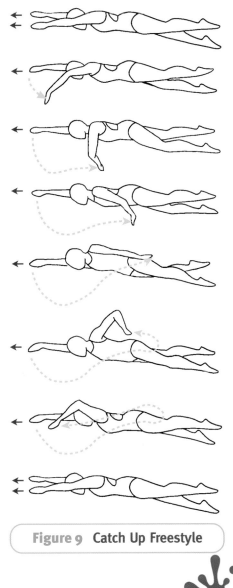

Figure 9 Catch Up Freestyle

47

Step 4: This sequence continues as one arm "catches up" to the other at the front of the stroke. Breathing is performed as needed, toward the moving arm, as the hand accelerates to the back of the stroke. Roll your face to the side to get a new breath. Keep the reaching arm extended and aligned with the shoulder as you inhale. Return your face to the water as your arm passes over the water.

Step 5: Continue for several lengths of the pool. Feel the momentum of each arm stroke as you press back on the water, accelerating through the pull, then push to full extension. Notice that there is always one arm leading and one arm stroking.

DRILL FEEDBACK CHART

Problem	Modification
My arm gets stuck underwater at the end of the stroke.	Begin the stroke by moving the hand, while the elbow remains still and high. Your hand should pass your elbow and extend to a straight arm position at the back, enabling you to clear the water.
I'm not moving.	Position your hands to press back on the water, not down toward the bottom of the pool. Pull then push the water toward your feet, accelerating through the stroke.
My arm sinks when I breathe.	When turning, breathe, reach forward with extended arm instead of pressing down.

All Thumbs Drill

10

THE PURPOSE OF THIS DRILL
- Learning to avoid over-reaching to the center at entry
- Practicing aligned extension
- Initiating the arm stroke from a position of strength

HOW TO DO THIS DRILL

Step 1: On land we point at things using our "pointer finger". Try it. Notice that this is largely a hand only position, and that the rest of the arm is not involved in the pointing motion. In swimming, because the purpose of pointing is to align our stroke forward, we use the whole arm. To best accomplish this, we have to learn to point with our thumbs.

Step 2: Standing in the water, extend your arm fully in front of you. Use your thumb to point to the far end of the pool. Notice when you point with your thumb, your shoulder, the inside of your elbow, and your thumb all align and aim forward. There is no bending at the wrist or elbow that makes a swimmer over-reach to the center, aim off course. Notice how your fingers are pitched outward, creating a wonderful paddle to catch water.

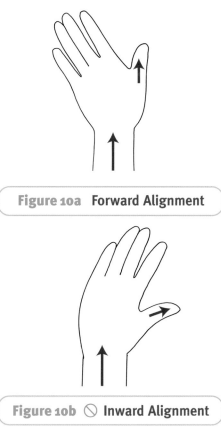

Figure 10a **Forward Alignment**

Figure 10b ⊘ **Inward Alignment**

Step 3: Now try it while swimming. While your arm enters the water and extends forward, point in the direction you are going with your thumbs. Reach to full extension by pushing your elbow and wrist in a straight line. Notice the alignment: shoulder, the inside of your elbow, and your thumb all line up straight ahead. You should feel like you are almost gliding forward directly toward your destination. Swim, thumbs leading to the far end of the pool.

Step 4: Continue to practice beginning your stroke aligned forward with your thumbs. Pitch your fingertips and palm downward, your thumb slightly lower than your pinkie. Feel the water against your fingertips take hold of the water like a handle. Move your body forward past your hand. Notice that when you begin the stroke from a well aligned position, you are able to feel more of a "handle" on the water.

Step 5: Practice more, beginning each new stroke from this position of strength with your thumbs leading. Feel the length of your stroke increase. Feel yourself move through the water farther with each stroke as you access more power.

DRILL FEEDBACK CHART

Problem	Modification
It feels awkward.	It probably feels much wider than you are used to. Remember, over-reaching to the center at entry is a big contributor to shoulder pain in swimming. Practice more. Align your reaching arm and thumb with the line on the bottom of the pool.
I don't feel the water against my fingertips.	Adjust the pitch of your hand. Keeping your thumb forward, allow the tips of your fingers to enter the water slightly before the heel of your hand. Slide your hand into the water, and forward as far as it will go.
I can't feel the alignment.	Push your elbows forward to align with your thumb. Maintain your "downhill" floating position.

Sculling

11

THE PURPOSE OF THIS DRILL
* Developing "feel" for the water
* Learning to hold on to the water
* Practicing changing hand pitch

HOW TO DO THIS DRILL
Step 1: Standing in shoulder-deep water, position your hands completely underwater, palms facing each other, about 24 inches apart. Hold your elbows firmly against your body. Sweep your hands towards each other. Just before they meet, sweep your hands down and back away from each other about 24 inches apart. Notice your hands have gone from a thumbs-up to a thumbs-down position.

Step 2: Upon reaching the widest point, again sweep your hands down and around until they are moving towards each other. Notice that your hands have gone from a thumbs-down position to a thumbs-up position. Continue this action until you feel you are tracing a sideways figure eight with each hand.

Step 3: You should be feeling that your hands are holding something of substance. Some swimmers describe the feeling of holding gelatin, others refer to pressing against something solid. Hold on to this substance in both directions, and as you turn the corners of your figure eight. This is sculling.

Step 4: Now lay in the water, face down, in a hand lead position. Accompanied by a light flutter kick, begin sculling with your arms extended. Adjust your hands so they remain completely submerged. Press outward with your thumbs down, and inward with your thumbs up. Hold on to the water throughout the sculling action. Attempt to create forward motion for 30 seconds.

Step 5: In the same floating position, move your hands under your belly, and using your sculling action, attempt to create forward motion in this position for 30 seconds.

Step 6: In the same floating position, move your hand to your sides, and using your sculling action, attempt to create forward motion in this position for 30 seconds.

Step 7: Once you have developed the ability to hold on to the water while sculling, try it when swimming freestyle. As your arm accelerates from front to back, feel the elongated sculling action. Hold on to the water throughout the whole path of the stroke. Adjust your hand as it sweeps through the stroke to maintain your hold on the water.

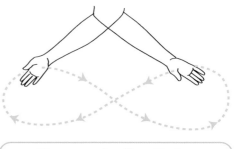

Figure 11 Sculling Motion

DRILL FEEDBACK CHART

Problem	Modification
I don't feel a thick substance in my hands.	Make sure your hands are completely submerged in the water. Use a quicker sweep. Hold your wrists firm. Experiment with pitching your hands slightly downward from the wrist.
I don't move anywhere.	Use a quicker sweep in both directions. Avoid pressing the water inward and outward on the same path. Trace a figure eight.
The scull at my sides doesn't work.	Make sure that your elbows are not moving too much. Hold them firm and press outward and inward quickly with your hands.

12 Fist Freestyle

THE PURPOSE OF THIS DRILL
- Learning to feel the water with the forearm
- Understanding the importance of a stable, high elbow
- Appreciating the role of the hand

HOW TO DO THIS DRILL

Step 1: Push off the wall preparing to do regular freestyle. Before the first stroke, form closed fists with each hand.

Step 2: Start the arm stroke. At first it may seem impossible to make forward progress without the paddle of your open hand. Keep sweeping through the path of the stroke, positioning your arm so your forearm works as your paddle to press against the water. To achieve this, you must keep your elbows high and stable, and to move your fists past your elbows.

Step 3: Use the whole length of the stroke, front to back. Align the entry. Keep your elbows high. Accelerate the underwater stroke. Adapt your stroke to the handless paddle. Continue to the other end of the pool.

Step 4: Now push off again, this time with open hands. Swim regular freestyle, using your hand as well as your forearm to press against the water. Align your entry. Keep your elbow high. Accelerate your stroke.

Step 5:
Continue alternating lengths of fist and open hand freestyle until you are feeling the water with a paddle that includes both your hand and your forearm.

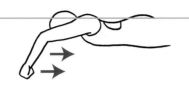

Figure 12a **Fist Freestyle Accessing Forearm**

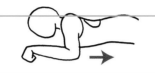

Figure 12b ⊘ **Fist Freestyle with Dropped Elbow**

DRILL FEEDBACK CHART

Problem	Modification
I am not moving.	Reposition your forearm so when your arm moves through the stroke, it quickly becomes perpendicular to the surface of the water.
I am feeling a lot of bubbles.	Entering the water with your fist will bring more air down into the water than your open hand. Perform the entry gently, and extend fully before you start the underwater arm stroke. Leave the bubbles behind as you change directions when your arm begins to press back on the water.
My elbows keep moving.	Try sticking your elbows out through the beginning and middle of the underwater arm stroke, as if trying to nudge someone. Hold them there while you move your hand past them.

RECOVERY DRILLS

Although there are many effective styles of freestyle recovery, they all have common aspects of technique. They all release the water. Each balances the stroking arm. All of them use a relaxed hand that is higher than the shoulder. The goal of the following freestyle recovery drills is to develop a recovery that maximizes rest while complementing the rest of the stroke.

13 Floppy Hand

THE PURPOSE OF THIS DRILL
* Practicing a relaxed recovery
* Learning to rest the arm during recovery
* Maintaining a high elbow recovery

HOW TO DO THIS DRILL
Step 1: Push off the wall and begin to do the "Catch Up" drill. As one arm remains reaching, the other will perform the underwater stroke. When the stroking arm reaches full extension to the rear, deliberately relax that hand.

Step 2: To transition to recovery, lift your elbow and slide you hand out of the water. It should feel as if you are pulling it out of your front pocket. Once your hand is clear of the water, your elbow should remain higher than your hand throughout its path over the water.

Step 3: Perform the recovery in slow motion focusing on relaxing your hand the whole time. As your arm travels toward the front, begin shaking your hand gently. Your hand should feel floppy and relaxed, as if you have no bones in your wrist. Your fingertips, hand and forearm should hang loosely from your elbow, pointing down toward the surface of the water, not forward. It should feel as though there is a puppet string pulling your elbow up, and everything else is dangling from it.

Step 4: When your recovering hand nears the front, flop it forward into the water. Your elbow should enter the water after the hand. When you have achieved the full extended position, begin stroking with the other arm.

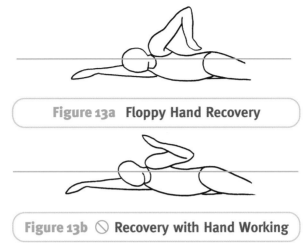

Figure 13a Floppy Hand Recovery

Figure 13b ⊘ Recovery with Hand Working

Step 5: Continue shaking your floppy hand during each slow motion recovery. Allow your hand to hang loosely from your elbow as it travels over the water and back to the front. Let your elbow follow your hand back into the water in front. Practice for several lengths of the pool.

DRILL FEEDBACK CHART

Problem	Modification
My hand carries water into the recovery.	Remember to push the water back in the direction you came from. Avoid lifting it up. The stroke should finish by your hip.
My hand isn't floppy.	Raise your elbow to begin the recovery and allow your hand and forearm to hang loosely from it throughout the time over the water.
There isn't time to get my hand to be floppy.	Perform the recovery in slow motion. There is no hurry. Focus on the over-the-water part of the stroke. As in the "Catch Up" drill, the other arm should wait until your recovering arm finishes.

 Shark Fin

THE PURPOSE OF THIS DRILL
- Practicing a relaxed, high elbow recovery
- Achieving a high elbow recovery by floating on your side
- Practicing the release of the water

HOW TO DO THIS DRILL

Step 1: Float in the water on your side, the arm near the surface at your side, and the other arm extended in front. Kick productively. To breathe, maintain core stability and roll towards your back, breathe, then roll back to your original side position.

Step 2: While maintaining a continuous kick, slide the hand at your side up to your waist, raising your elbow up to a point, like a shark's fin. Your elbow should be pointing to the sky. Hold this "shark fin" position for five seconds, allowing your hand to hang relaxed. Slide your hand back down to full extension at your side.

Step 3: Repeat this action with the same arm, trying to make the most impressive shark fin possible. Notice that to make the highest shark fin, you have to float completely on that side of your body, and allow the other side of your body to float low. Return your arm to your side.

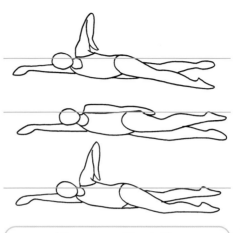

Step 4: After ten shark fins, then switch sides. Continue to the other end of the pool.

Figure 14   Shark Fin

DRILL FEEDBACK CHART

Problem	Modification
It is hard to get my elbow up.	Make sure you are floating on your side. Unless you are unusually flexible, the human shoulder cannot make a shark fin unless you are floating on your side.
I am sinking.	Try kicking a bit more to produce more forward movement.
My hand is not relaxed.	Practice more. Get comfortable on your side. Lift from the elbow.

BREATHING DRILLS

Integrating the act of breathing into the stroke is a challenge. By timing the breath to the natural roll of the stroke, a swimmer can breathe rhythmically while continuing the forward line of the stroke. The goal of the following freestyle breathing drills is to address issues of timing and alignment, and, to learn to use the core for better breathing technique.

15 Inhale Arm/Exhale Arm

THE PURPOSE OF THIS DRILL
- Learning the correct timing of the freestyle breathing
- Using a regular breathing pattern
- Maintaining a relaxed, rhythmic stroke with breathing

HOW TO DO THIS DRILL
Step 1: Choose a side that you will turn toward for breathing. The arm on that side will be called your "inhale arm". The other arm will be called your "exhale arm".

Step 2: Standing in waist deep water, bow forward until your face is submerged. Extend your arms forward, aligned with your shoulders to do the freestyle arm stroke in the standing position. Do several strokes, saying to your self "inhale", as you are stroking underwater with the "inhale arm", and saying, "exhale", as you are stroking with the "exhale arm".

Step 3: Now try to actually get a breath. Stroke first with your "inhale arm". As you begin to press back on the water, start turning your face to the side toward the "inhale arm". Turn your face until your mouth clears the water, but keep your lower cheek in the water. Inhale as your hand reaches the back of the stroke. Inhale deeply through your mouth. Then, as the "inhale arm" returns over the water to the front, allow your face to follow it, arriving back into the water by the time the "inhale arm" passes your shoulder. Look at the bottom of the pool.

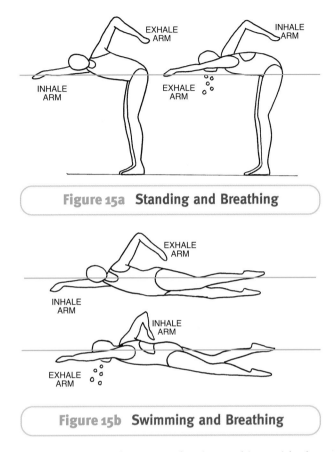

Figure 15a **Standing and Breathing**

Figure 15b **Swimming and Breathing**

Step 4: When your face returns to the water, begin stroking with the "exhale arm". As you begin to press back on the water, look down at the bottom of the pool and exhale. Exhale through your mouth and nose. You should see an abundance of bubbles as you exhale. Continue exhaling throughout the length of the stroke, and as the "exhale arm" returns over the water to the front.

Step 5: As your "exhale arm" passes your shoulder, again begin stroking with the "inhale arm". Continue stroking rhythmically, inhaling with the one-arm stroke, and exhaling with the other. Maintain the full length of each stroke. Do a quick, deep inhale through your mouth. Do a long, thorough exhale from your mouth and nose, producing bubbles. Practice until you can breathe rhythmically with the rhythm of the stroke.

Step 6: Now try breathing while swimming freestyle. Start slowly. Stroke several times saying to your self "inhale" and "exhale" as the designated arm strokes through the water. Then try turning your head toward the "inhale arm" as it strokes. Turn to the point that your mouth clears the water but your cheek remains connected to the water. Inhale as your arm reaches the back of the stroke. Then, allow your face to turn back into the water, following your "inhale arm" as it recovers back to the front. Exhale as the "exhale arm" strokes.

Step 7: Practice several times then rest. Practice again. Be patient and set the rhythm of your arm stroke to your inhale and exhale.

DRILL FEEDBACK CHART

Problem	Modification
I lose the rhythm after a few strokes.	It takes practice. Keep each stroke long. Cue your inhale and your exhale with the movements of the corresponding arm. Stop when you get off time. Rest, then start again.
I don't seem to have time to inhale.	Make sure you are exhaling thoroughly before you turn to inhale. There is not time to both exhale and inhale when you are turned to the side. If you spend the time exhaling, you will miss the opportunity to inhale. Exhale thoroughly while the "exhale arm" is stroking.
I run out of air before it is time to inhale again.	Make sure you are exhaling thoroughly before you turn to inhale. There is not time to both exhale and inhale when you are turned to the side. If you spend the time exhaling, you will miss the opportunity to inhale. Exhale thoroughly while the "exhale arm" is stroking.

The Weightless Arm   16

THE PURPOSE OF THIS DRILL
* Maintaining the full length of the arm stroke while breathing
* Learning the correct timing of the freestyle breathing
* Using your core to breathe, not just your head

HOW TO DO THIS DRILL
Step 1: Push off the wall for freestyle. Achieve a firm core and look at the bottom of the pool. Swim to the far end of the pool. Begin swimming freestyle. Establish a relaxed stroke and regular breathing rhythm. Inhale with one arm, exhale with the other.

Step 2: When you have reached about the halfway mark to the other end of the pool, at the exact point when your mouth clears the water to inhale, freeze in that position. Identify precisely where the arm is that you are turned away from when breathing. Has it left the fully extended position? Is it under your chest? If the answer to either of these questions is "yes", you have a heavy arm. As this heavy arm presses down on the water in an attempt to lift you up to breathe, it works like an anchor. When your arm sinks, you lose half of your next stroke that could have moved you forward in the water.

Step 3: To avoid a heavy arm, float on your side, with your breathing side higher in the water. Extend your lower arm fully in front of you. Position the higher arm at your side. Begin a gentle flutter kick. Holding your core firm, roll your face, shoulder and hip as a unit back until your mouth clears the water. Inhale. Roll back down. Practice several times, maintaining the position of your extended position of your lower arm throughout your roll and inhale.

Step 4: Now, try it while stroking. Again float on your side, breathing side high. Stroke through the water with your lower side arm, and recover over the water with your higher side arm. Once you have switched floating sides and switched arm positions, prepare to breathe on the next stroke. As your arms again begin to switch positions, hold your core firm, roll your face, shoulders and hips up in unison towards the stroking arm. By the time the stroking arm reaches the back of the stroke, you should be floating on your other side with your mouth clear of the water to inhale.

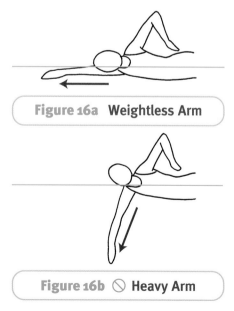

Figure 16a   Weightless Arm

Figure 16b   ⊘ Heavy Arm

Step 5: Notice the position of your lower arm. It should be fully extended throughout your

breath, reaching toward the far end of the pool, fairly close to the surface of the water...as if weightless. Practice again. Continue practicing until you can inhale as the lower arm reaches forward, instead of pressing down.

Step 6: Once you are comfortable with this breathing position, begin to swim regular freestyle. Go slowly and focus on reaching forward with your lower arm as you roll your face, shoulder and hip up to the high side for each breath. Keep reaching forward throughout your inhale. Practice until you achieve a weightless reaching arm.

DRILL FEEDBACK CHART

Problem	Modification
My mouth does not clear the water to breathe.	Roll the low hip and shoulder down more. Keep kicking when you are breathing.
My reaching arm is still heavy.	Slow down your stroke. Practice the 12 Kick Switch and Catch Up drills to get comfortable with this floating position.
I don't seem to have time to fit the breath into my stroke.	Focus on initiating the roll early in the stroke. Keep practicing. This is a difficult skill.

17 Temple Press

THE PURPOSE OF THIS DRILL
- Practicing the correct head alignment while breathing
- Learning to use a "low profile" breathing technique
- Experiencing the bow wave when inhaling

HOW TO DO THIS DRILL
Step 1: Stand in waist deep water. Bow forward at the waist and submerge your face in the water. Look at the bottom of the pool. Extend your arms in front of you on the surface of the water. Bring one arm back toward your hip underwater, and turn to that side, as if breathing in freestyle. Freeze in that position. What parts of your head are connected to the water? Your jaw bone? Your cheek? How about your temple?

Step 2: Adjust your head position so that your temple is pressing down on the water. Notice that by doing so your cheek and your jaw bone automatically connect to the water. Your mouth might not clear the water as much as you are used to. That is fine.

Step 3: Now begin to swim regular freestyle. Roll up to breathe and reach forward with your lower arm. While turned for the inhale, press your temple into the water. Feel that your cheek and your jaw bone connect to the water as well. Notice that as you are moving forward during the breath, the water parts around your head, like it does at the bow of a moving boat. With your temple pressed into the water,

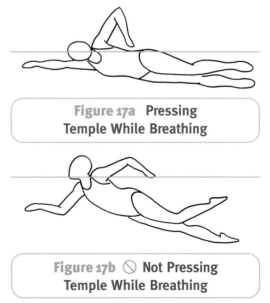

Figure 17a Pressing Temple While Breathing

Figure 17b ⃠ **Not Pressing Temple While Breathing**

this "bow wave" will create a sort of pocket of air for you to inhale, even if your mouth is very close to the water.

Step 4: Continue swimming, using the low profile breathing technique by pressing your temple into the water, and breathing within the "bow wave".

DRILL FEEDBACK CHART

Problem	Modification
I can't get my temple down when swimming freestyle.	Work on your floating position. Start by looking at the bottom of the pool. Get your chest down and float "downhill".
My face doesn't clear the water.	Roll the breathing side hip and shoulder up more, and the other side hip and shoulder down more.
I am getting water in my mouth.	Create more forward motion with a stronger kick. The more forward momentum you have, the greater that "bow wave" will be, making the water go around you, not in your mouth.

18 Dead Arm Freestyle

THE PURPOSE OF THIS DRILL
- Feeling the core involvement in breathing
- Reaching forward while breathing
- Experiencing the correct timing of the breathing

HOW TO DO THIS DRILL

Step 1: Push off the wall as if preparing to swim freestyle. Bring one arm to your side and hold it there motionless. Engage your core tension.

Step 2: Swim freestyle with the other arm only. Before each stroke, focus on aligning your moving arm forward, directly in front of your shoulder. When you stroke, maintain a high elbow position, and use the full length of each stroke to accelerate through. Pull then push from front to back.

Step 3: Breathe towards the side with the motionless arm. Without moving your head independently, turn to breathe using your hips

Figure 18 Breathing Toward the Dead Arm

and shoulders to initiate your roll to breathe. Time your inhale to begin when the moving arm is reaching for the front, just as your finger tips touch the water. Keep reaching forward throughout the inhale.

Step 4: As you inhale, you should be able to see the shoulder on your breathing side out of the water. As you return your face to the water, feel that shoulder and same side hip roll down.

Step 5: Continue swimming with one arm to the end of the pool, focusing on breathing with your body roll. Switch arms. Repeat. Continue practicing until you can achieve balanced breathing by rolling with a firm core.

DRILL FEEDBACK CHART

Problem	Modification
I can't get a breath.	Roll the hip and shoulder down with the stroking arm. You won't be able to get a breath if you are flat.
I have to stretch my neck and raise my chin to get a breath.	Establish and maintain a "downhill" float. Accelerate your one arm pull toward your hip. Kick more.
It feels awkward.	This is an advanced drill! It will take time to master it. Practice more.

LEVERAGE DRILLS

Using leverage gives freestlyers an advantage. Instead of swimming flat, and depending on the small muscles of the arm, swimmers can use the body to roll into and out of each stroke. Doing so accesses more power from the core. By engaging the large muscles of the core it is possible to travel more distance per stroke, with the same amount of energy. The freestyle becomes more productive and more sustainable. In addition, using core leverage avoids injury to vulnerable shoulder joints. Long term flat freestyle is responsible for many swimmers being out of the water for extended periods of time, with bursitis or rotator cuff problems. By using core leverage, the shoulders can be spared of the entire burden of freestyle. The goal of the following freestyle leverage drills is to create a more sustainable and injury-free freestyle by using available leverage to the fullest.

19 Three Stroke Switch Freestyle

THE PURPOSE OF THIS DRILL
- Practicing the roll into and out of the stroke
- Accessing your core strength
- Transferring power from the core to the limbs

HOW TO DO THIS DRILL
Step 1: Push off the wall preparing to do freestyle, core engaged, perform three freestyle strokes (one arm = one stroke), accompanied by a productive flutter kick. As your arm approaches your hip on the third stroke, roll onto your side and float and kick with the arm that just finished stroking at your side, the other arm fully extended. The arm at your side should be closer to the surface, and the arm lower in the water should be extended over your head. Holding this position, do six good kicks (one leg = one kick).

Step 2: With your sixth kick, roll your higher hip and shoulder down into the water as the arm at your side recovers over the water to the front, and the reaching arm begins stroking. Do three more freestyle strokes. Continue kicking the through the whole process. Breathing should be done to the side during the three strokes. During the kick-only phase, the face should remain mostly submerged, ear against the lower shoulder.

Step 3: Continue doing three strokes, kicking the whole time, and then six more kicks in the side position until you reach the far end of the pool.

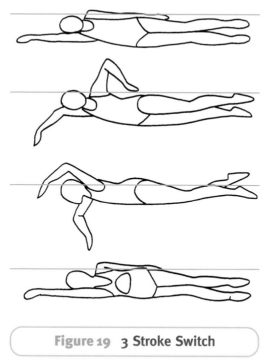

Figure 19   **3 Stroke Switch**

71

Notice that when changing from the side kicking phase to the stroking phase, the recovering arm travels easily to the front with leverage of the hip roll. Notice too, at the same time, that the leading arm goes easily into the next stroke, also aided by the hip roll.

Step 4: Keep practicing. Once you are comfortable with the 3 strokes and 6 kicks rhythm, change to 3 strokes and 3 kicks. Then, work on incorporating a "switch" between each stroke. Notice that what you are doing is almost identical to regular freestyle...a very long, efficient freestyle.

Step 5: Once you are able to roll with each stroke, begin swimming regular freestyle rolling into and out of each stroke, as you did in the drill.

DRILL FEEDBACK CHART

Problem	Modification
I go crooked.	Employ core stability and align your leading arm with the line on the bottom of the pool.
I don't roll as much in the three strokes as I do changing to the side kicking phase.	Slow down your strokes. Allow time to roll.
It seems that rolling all the way over to my side is too far.	Remember, this is a drill, where the point is to learn to roll. The action is a bit exaggerated to make the point. In regular swimming you actually roll to the point where you balance on the top of your hip bone and your armpit.

The Pendulum Effect

THE PURPOSE OF THIS DRILL
* Understanding the relationship between the recovering arm and the stroking arm
* Feeling acceleration during the switch
* Maintaining balance

HOW TO DO THIS DRILL
Step 1: Float in the water on your side, the arm near the surface at your side, and the other arm extended in front. Kick productively. Slide the hand at your side up to your waist, raising your elbow up to a point, like in the Shark Fin drill. To breathe, maintain your core stability and roll towards your back, breathe, then roll back to your original side position.

Step 2: Hold this position for five seconds, continuing to kick. Notice that at in this position, on your side with one arm extended, and the other arm at its highest point in recovery, neither arm is producing any forward motion.

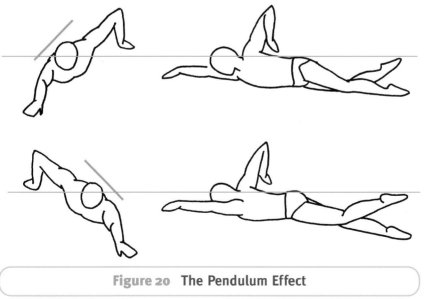

Figure 20   The Pendulum Effect

Step 3: Stroke through with your extended arm as you finish your recovery with arm over the water. Find the same floating position on the other side. Your lower arm should be extended, and your higher arm should be making a shark fin. Again hold for five seconds, continuing to kick.

Step 4: Switch to the other side again. Continue to the far end of the pool, switching to the identical position with your arms on either side, and holding for five seconds before switching. Notice that as you switch arm positions, your hips switch sides too. Notice too that each switch gathers speed from beginning to end.

Step 5: Do another length, this time holding only for three seconds before switching sides. Feel the beginning and the end of each switch. Like the extremes of a pendulum's swing, the motion starts slowly and gathers speed, continuously from side to side.

Step 6: Do another length, this time holding for only one second before switching sides. Feel the pendulum swing and gather speed with each switch. Notice that while one arm reaching and the other out of the water in recovery, neither arm is moving you forward, yet you are still moving forward.

Step 7: Continue to practice, feeling the pendulum effect with each stroke. Focus on using your hips to add power to the switch of your arm positions. Feel your stroke cover more distance with no more effort.

DRILL FEEDBACK CHART

Problem	Modification
I can't keep my elbow in a shark fin.	Your opposite shoulder should be at its lowest point in the water, allowing you to point your recovering elbow toward the sky. Relax your hand and let it hang from your higher elbow.
My hips don't add power.	Your hips are probably floating flat. Start in the side floating position, with your shoulder and your hip on the recovering side high. Each time you switch, make sure to achieve the side floating position with shoulders as well as your hips.
My kick stops when I switch sides.	Maintaining a continuous kick is important in this drill, and it is important in the full stroke. Blank spots can interfere with the pendulum effect. Use your kick to add power to the switch.

Hip Skating

21

THE PURPOSE OF THIS DRILL
- Observing the role of the hips
- Learning to use leverage from the core
- Mastering switching from hip to hip

HOW TO DO THIS DRILL

Step 1: The rhythm of ice skating resembles the rhythm of swimming freestyle. As one side of the body balances, the other is applying force. To go faster, the ice skater does not do shorter, choppier movements. Instead, each stride is extended, using leverage from the hips to produce motion. Try it. Attach an imaginary ice skate to each of your hips on the bone you can feel at the highest and forward most points of your pelvis.

Step 2: Now, push off the wall, face down in the water, preparing to do freestyle, firm core, aligned, floating "downhill". Glide forward on the imaginary hip skates. As you get ready to take your first stroke with your right arm, shift your weight toward your right hip, so you are balancing on that skate only, then start

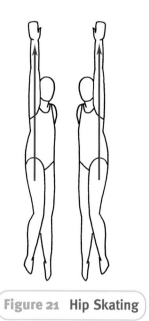

Figure 21 **Hip Skating**

the stroke. As the right arm approaches the end of the stroke, switch your weight to your left hip skate, allowing the right hip to rise, while the left arm starts its stroke, and the right arm recovers.

Step 3: Continue skating on your hips, right, then left, then right, then left. Notice how shifting your weight from skate to skate sends power upward through your core to your arm stroke.

DRILL FEEDBACK CHART

Problem	Modification
I can't balance on my hips and float "downhill" at the same time.	The "downhill" position corrects your floating position. Start with that. Balancing on your hips drives your stroke. Focus on core stability in both ways. Be patient and keep practicing to achieve both skills.
My head is moving side to side with my hips, even when I am not breathing.	Relax the muscles in your neck. On the strokes when you are not breathing, allow your hips and shoulders to roll while your head remains still. Keep looking at the bottom of the pool. It is as if your head was an independent object, floating in front of your body.
If I glide too long I just stop.	Yes. So, your task is to identify the point just before you slow down and switch your weight to the other hip to start your next stroke then. This will make the most of your momentum.

COORDINATION DRILLS

There are many elements of the stroke technique that make up freestyle work in combination to produce coordinated forward motion. Each element affects another, together contributing to a unified, productive freestyle. The goal of the following coordination drills is to learn to bring multiple freestyle skills together into a coordinated effort for the most productive freestyle.

Heads Up Freestyle

THE PURPOSE OF THIS DRILL
* Learning to grab the water and stroke back
* Using a continuous stroke
* Matching the kick to the arm stroke

HOW TO DO THIS DRILL

Step 1: A lifeguard swimming to a person in trouble approaches the victim using a modified head up freestyle to keep his or her eyes on the victim and get there as quickly as possible. Likewise, a designated sprinter for a waterpolo team races to gain control of the ball, using modified head up freestyle to watch the ball to be captured. Try Heads Up Freestyle. Focus your eyes on a point at the far end of the pool and get there as fast as you can.

Step 2: Stroke quickly, keeping your chin low in the water, and your eyes focused forward. Keep your head up the whole time. Notice that to keep your head up, when your hand enters in front, you must engage the water immediately with your fingertips, palm and forearm, and stroke continuously. Your stroke becomes shorter, and your recovery becomes wider. Notice too that while it is possible to keep your head up by pressing down on the water with your hands, you limit your forward motion by doing so.

Step 3: Continue swimming head up, engaging the water immediately with each stroke. Keep your elbows high. Accelerate to the back with each short, quick stroke. Notice that by pressing back on the water to go forward, your head stays above the water without pushing down. Grab hold of the water aggressively and move closer to your target with each stroke.

Step 4: With your head up, your body position is not ideal in the water. To manage this "uphill" swimming position, stabilize your core and kick actively, coordinating your kick to your arm stroke. Although the rate of the kick is quicker than the rate of the arm stroke, one kick should match each arm entry. As one arm enters in front, kick down with one foot. Notice that by coordinating the rhythm of your kick to the arm entry, your kick also matches the finish of the stroke by the other arm. Doing so creates additional forward motion, but also lift and balance to the whole stroke.

Figure 22 Heads Up Freestyle

Step 5: Continue toward your target. Notice that even from this disadvantageous swimming position, you can move forward well when all the parts of the stroke are coordinated and working together. Rest, then try it again.

Step 6: Now try swimming regular freestyle with your face in the water. Use the same quick stroke rate as you did in the Heads Up drill. Press back on the water keeping your elbows high. Match the

downbeat of your kick to the point when your hand first takes hold of the water in front. Feel the lift and balance in your stroke.

Step 7: Rest, then alternate several lengths of Heads Up Freestyle and regular freestyle.

DRILL FEEDBACK CHART

Problem	Modification
I am struggling to keep my face up.	Stroke quickly and keep your elbows high as you start each stroke. Accelerate to the back of the stroke. Avoid pressing down on the water to stay up. Instead, move yourself forward by pressing back on the water. Kick with each arm entry.
It is very tiring.	Yes, swimming "uphill" is as tiring as running "uphill". And to make forward progress, all parts of the body must work together.
It hurts my neck.	Make sure you are balancing on your chest. By doing so, you will not have to raise your chin so much to keep your face out of the water. If it continues to hurt after making this modification, just don't do it.

23 Horizontal Rope Climbing

THE PURPOSE OF THIS DRILL
* Utilizing the largest muscles possible
* Moving past your anchored hand
* Feeling efficient forward motion

HOW TO DO THIS DRILL
Step 1: Think about how a person climbs a rope. Hand over hand, the climber uses one hand to grasp the rope at a point higher than the body, while the other hand holds the body steady at the previous advance. When the reaching hand has a good grip on the rope, the climber moves his or her body past that reaching hand, while the lower hand then becomes the one that reaches to a higher point. This is exactly how the best swimming is. Rather than churning the water madly, efficient swimmers reach and grab hold of the water in front of them, then move their bodies beyond that point, hand over hand.

Step 2: String a rope from one end of the pool to the other. Use the lane line hooks at each end of the pool to secure your rope, but allow slack so that most of the rope floats about one foot under the surface. Avoid using lane lines for this drill. They can snap without warning, and are very expensive to replace.

Step 3: Once your rope is in place, take a big breath and float face down in the water over the rope. With the image of the rope climber in mind, reach as far forward as you can with one hand and take hold of the rope. Keeping your elbow high, pull your body forward

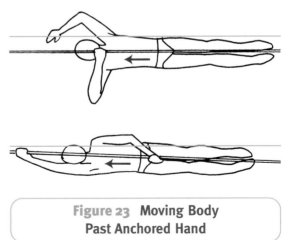

Figure 23 Moving Body Past Anchored Hand

past the reaching hand, until your arm is straight and at your hip. At the same time, use the other hand to reach to a father point. Continue, arm over arm, moving your body farther along the rope. When you have to breathe, lift your face out of the water gently, then return to your face down position.

Step 4: Continue to the far end of the pool. Feel your body advance through the water past your reaching hand. Practice several times. Then try regular freestyle, without the rope. Take hold of the water, then move yourself past that point with each stroke. Climb through the water. This is the essence of efficient swimming.

DRILL FEEDBACK CHART

Problem	Modification
This is hard!	Avoid dropping your elbows. High elbows give you more leverage to lift your body past your reaching hand.
My legs wag back and forth.	Employ a stable core. You can also kick gently.
I thought I was supposed to align my reach with my shoulders, not to the center of my body like with the rope.	Very good! This is true, and it is one of the shortcomings of this drill. Try to ignore this aspect and focus on how you advance past your reaching hand.

24 Freestyle with Dolphin

THE PURPOSE OF THIS DRILL
- Coordinating the kick and the arm stroke
- Setting the stroke rhythm to the kick
- Using the momentum of the kick to benefit the arm stroke

HOW TO DO THIS DRILL

Step 1: Push off the wall preparing to do freestyle, arms extended, core engaged. Do six to twelve good dolphin kicks. Focus on producing a rhythmic kick with a compact, yet powerful downbeat, while your feet stay connected to the water. For this drill, it is important to keep your head stable, and not bouncing a lot.

Step 2: Once you have established a strong, rhythmic kick, begin a freestyle arm stroke. Time your kick so you are producing one kick for each single arm stroke. Note: this is different than butterfly stroke rhythm. Once you have matched a kick to each arm stroke, time the downbeat of each kick to happen at precisely the moment that your hand strikes the water in front.

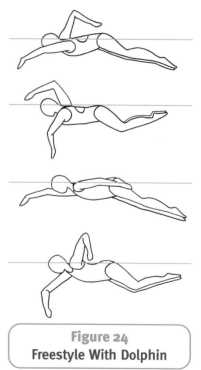

Step 3: Continue to the other end of the pool, focusing on coordinating these two actions. Rest and repeat until the freestyle arms and dolphin kick are well coordinated with a sustainable rhythm. Notice that when the downbeat of your dolphin kick is timed to the entry of your hand in front, that you reach forward with more momentum, encouraging you to extend farther for longer. Notice too, that although you are focusing timing your kick to the reaching arm, that the same kick is also assisting the stroking arm, assisting you in accelerating to the back of your stroke.

Figure 24
Freestyle With Dolphin

Step 4: Repeat the drill. Quicken the rhythm of your kick. Match your arm stroke to that quicker rhythm. As you plant your hand in the water in front, plant your feet in the water to the rear.

Step 5: Now try the same coordination using a flutter kick. While it is common to use more than one flutter kick per arm, make sure that one of your kicks matches the entry of your hand, and simultaneously assists the fast finish of the other hand, for every stroke that you take. Practice for several lengths of the pool.

DRILL FEEDBACK CHART

Problem	Modification
My dolphin kick seems out of alignment.	If you are doing this correctly, your hips will roll, as they should in freestyle, making the dolphin kick not exactly up and down. That is okay. The point of the drill is to match the rhythm of the kick to the arms.
When I use the flutter kick, I am using the same side arm and leg to do the simultaneous motion.	This is fine. It really depends on the number of flutter kicks you do per stroke. The average is three kicks per arm, however, many swimmers do two or four. Some even do two on one side and three on the other. This timing can be done successfully using the same side arm and leg, as well as the opposite arm and leg.
My freestyle arm stroke turns into butterfly arms when I use the dolphin kick.	Avoid diving your head down as your arms enter. Use a more compact kick, and reach forward upon entry, not down. Kick once per arm, not twice like in butterfly.

25 Bilateral Breathing

THE PURPOSE OF THIS DRILL
- Coordinating the breathing with the body roll
- Developing a symmetrical roll
- Developing a symmetrical kick

HOW TO DO THIS DRILL

Step 1: Push off the wall preparing to do regular freestyle. Establish a good, continuous kick. Swim to the other end of the pool breathing toward the right side of the pool. Rest, then swim another length back to your starting point, facing the same side of the pool when you breathe. This will mean you are breathing to the other side of your body. Repeat until you are comfortable maintaining your alignment and kick, and rolling your body to get a breath on your right and left sides.

Step 2: Now, swim another length breathing every third stroke. Time your inhale to start at the same time as the entry of the hand you are breathing away from. Strike the water left, then right, then strike and breathe left. Strike the water right, then left, then strike and breathe right. Remember the Weightless Arm drill, and the Temple Press drill while you are perfecting this timing.

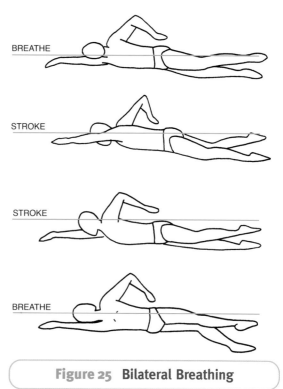

BREATHE

STROKE

STROKE

BREATHE

Figure 25 Bilateral Breathing

Step 3: Continue to practice breathing every third stroke for several lengths of the pool. One side may seem more natural to you than the other, just like one hand seems more natural when writing. Keep practicing trying to make your less natural side a mirror image of your natural side.

Step 4: Once you are comfortable with this timing, focus on your hip roll. Notice that with bilateral breathing, it is more even on both sides than when you breathe on just one side. Notice too, that your kick has fewer pauses in it, and it is more compact, especially during breathing. Finally, notice that your arm stroke is more symmetrical in depth, width and length with bilateral breathing.

Step 5: Practice for several lengths of the pool. Develop a balanced stroke by breathing on both sides.

DRILL FEEDBACK CHART

Problem	Modification
My neck hurts when I breathe to the left.	Remember to turn your body to breathe, not just your neck. Focus on rolling your right hip down when breathing on your left.
Breathing every third stroke seems too often for me.	Although breathing every third stroke is preferred by many swimmers, it may not be right for you as a regular swimming rhythm. However, it is still very beneficial as a drill to develop a symmetrical stroke and kick.
I lose the rhythm after a few strokes.	When you notice your rhythm is off, stop, rest, then begin again. Be persistent. It will pay off.

DRILLS FOR
BACKSTROKE

BODY POSITION DRILLS

Learning to float well on the back is the first step in being comfortable with the backstroke. Good spinal alignment and core tension not only improve comfort on the back, but can also contribute to an effective backstroke. The goal of the following drills for body position in backstroke is to experience positive backstroke floatation upon which a good backstroke can be built.

Float on Spine

26

THE PURPOSE OF THIS DRILL
- Achieving an advantageous backstroke floating position
- Feeling effective core tension and stability
- Being comfortable on the back

HOW TO DO THIS DRILL
Step 1: Lay horizontally in the water, face up, without attempting any forward motion, arms at sides, head leading.

Step 2: Focus on how your spine affects your floatation. First, round your spine so that your knees come up toward your chest, and your hips are low, as if you were sitting in the water. Notice that you have a hard time floating in this position. Your face may even submerge.

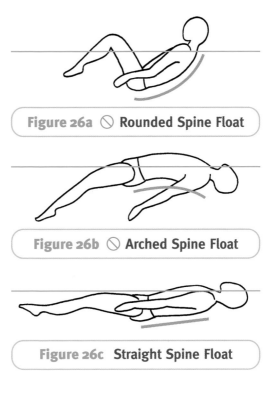

Figure 26a ⃠ **Rounded Spine Float**

Figure 26b ⃠ **Arched Spine Float**

Figure 26c **Straight Spine Float**

Step 3: Resume your horizontal position in the water, face up. Focus on your spine. Now, arch your back, so your belly button is the highest point of your body. Try to get it above the water. Notice that by doing so your face submerges, or nearly submerges in the water. Your legs may also sink.

Step 4: Again lay horizontally in the water, face up. Focus on your spine. Make it as absolutely straight as possible. This includes straightening the natural bends in the small of the back and at the neck. To accomplish this, rotate your pelvis forward, and press the back of your head into the water. Notice that in doing so, you contract your abdominal muscles, and actually relax your neck. Notice too that your body floats more horizontally. This is the advantageous floating position which you can build a good backstroke stroke upon.

Step 5: Practice several times until you achieve the feeling of balancing on your spine.

DRILL FEEDBACK CHART

Problem	Modification
My legs still sink.	If you have heavy legs, it is even more important to learn to rotate your pelvis forward. Contract your abdominal muscles, and float on your spine.
I'm not sure my spine is straight.	You can check it by standing against a wall and pressing every inch of your spine into the wall. Reach back and try to slide your hand between the wall and the small of your back. If you succeed, you need to rotate your pelvis more forward to close this gap. Check the same way behind your neck. No space should remain. Take time to analyze what muscles you are engaging to achieve your straight spine, then, do it in the water.
Doing this makes my hips higher than my belly button.	Yes, that is correct. You might feel sort of like an elongated banana in the front of your body. But in the backstroke, it is your spine that you float on, and that is what needs to be straight.

Water-Line Drill

27

THE PURPOSE OF THIS DRILL
- Finding correct head alignment
- Feeling the water-line around your face
- Relaxing the neck, shoulders and upper back

HOW TO DO THIS DRILL
Step 1: Lay horizontally in the water, face up, arms at sides, spine straight. Do not produce any forward motion.

Step 2: Now move your chin toward your chest until the surface of the water, or the "water-line" is just below your ear lobes. Notice that in this position, the muscles in your neck and shoulders are fully engaged. Your legs may also sink, and it will probably be difficult to maintain your floatation.

Step 3: Now lay horizontally in the water, face up, spine straight. Lift your chin and rock your head back, until your ears are completely submerged and you can see the water at the back of your head. The waterline will be at your eye brows and around your throat. Notice that in this position, the muscles in the back of your neck and upper back are engaged. Your float will probably not suffer, although you will feel probably quite stiff.

Step 4: Again lay horizontally in the water, face up, spine straight. Hold your chin neutral, as if you are looking at someone who is exactly the same height as you. The water-line will surround your face, from your hairline to the bottom of your chin. In this position, your ears will be submerged and your neck, shoulders and upper back will be relaxed, like when your head rests on a pillow. This is the correct head position for the back-stroke.

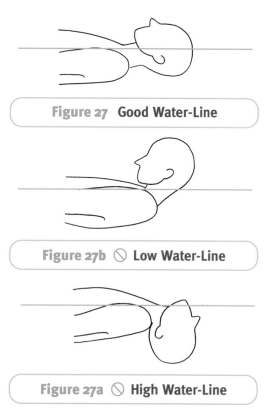

Figure 27 Good Water-Line

Figure 27b ⊘ Low Water-Line

Figure 27a ⊘ High Water-Line

DRILL FEEDBACK CHART

Problem	Modification
Water gets in my ears.	This is a problem that will be resolved when you add forward motion to the float in the next section. The water will then pass by your ears instead of going in them.
I seem to float better with my ears out of the water.	You might be achieving the needed abdominal contraction by lifting your upper body, rather than rotating your pelvis forward. It is important to use your pelvis to contract your abdominal muscles, because you need your upper body to stay aligned in the direction you are going.
I am not able to relax my neck.	Lower your shoulders. Float with your palms facing the surface of the water. Breathe in and out deeply. Practice letting the water hold your head.

28 Twelve Kick Switch Backstroke

THE PURPOSE OF THIS DRILL
- Maintaining a straight spine while moving
- Beginning to feel leverage from the core
- Identifying the longest backstroke position

HOW TO DO THIS DRILL

Step 1: Lay on your side in the water, with the arm closest to the surface at your side, and the arm closest to the bottom of the pool extended over your head. Achieve a straight spine, and good water-line.

Step 2: Begin a gentle but continuous flutter kick, which should also be directed side to side.

Step 3: Although your body is floating on its side, allow your face to float straight up, so it is completely out of the water. Relax your neck so your head feels like an independent object floating in front of your body. In this position, the shoulder of the arm at your side should be out of the water and closer to your cheek than your other arm is to the other cheek.

Step 4: Kick twelve times (each leg equals one kick).

Step 5: Just as you finish the last kick, bring the arm laying by your side straight over the water to an extended position over your head, and at the same time, bring the forward reaching arm through the water to your side, as you switch to the opposite side of your body to float. All the time maintain a straight spine and core stability.

Figure 28   12 Kick Switch Backstroke

Step 6: Kick twelve more kicks in this position. Repeat the switch with your arms and floating side. Continue to kick twelve times then switch until you reach the far end of the pool.

DRILL FEEDBACK CHART

Problem	Modification
I get a lot of water in my face.	Make sure your chin is neutral and that your spine is straight. But remember, the fact is that even excellent backstrokers get water in their face. However, the more momentum you produce, the more the water will go around you, instead of in your face.
My kick is aimed up and down.	Let the hip on the side with your arm extended be lower than the other hip.
I go crooked.	Align your extended arm straight and lock your elbow. Do this drill next to the side of the pool, or by a lane line to keep your bearings.

KICK DRILLS

An effective flutter kick is a significant part of an efficient backstroke. Although similar in its alternating motion to the flutter kick of freestyle, there are certain distinctions. Kicking well on the back requires employing leg muscles differently than humans commonly do for most land activities. The major force of the backstroke kick is upward, against gravity, making quick, compact kicking and good foot position extremely important. The goal of the following backstroke kicking drills is to address the unique issues of the backstroke kick that contribute to an effective and sustainable kicking technique.

Boiling Water Drill

THE PURPOSE OF THIS DRILL
- Learning to kick upward with force
- Feeling the water with your feet
- Developing a centralized kick

HOW TO DO THIS DRILL
Step 1: Stand in the water a bit more than waist deep. Hold one arm outstretched in front of you about twelve inches over the surface of the water. Now, drop your hand down with force into the water. Notice that the splash that occurs goes in all directions. Notice too the sound that your hand makes as it makes a hole in the water.

Step 2: Now, hold your arm outstretched about twelve inches under the surface of the water. Raise your hand up with force to about three inches under the surface of the water. Notice the water welling up, almost like water coming to a boil. Repeat this action, with more force, as if bringing the water to a full boil, without your hand ever reaching the surface of the water. This is what your feet do in a good backstroke kick.

Step 3: Try the same thing with your feet. Standing with your back supported at the side of the pool, bring your foot about twelve inches over the surface of the water and drop it down into the water. Notice the large splash. Listen to the distinct sound of your foot making a hole in the water. Now hold your foot twelve inches under the water, toes pointed, and force your foot up towards the surface, but don't allow any part of your foot to break the surface of the water. Make the water boil. Notice the feeling of the water against the top of your foot.

Step 4: Now lay horizontally in the water, face up, straight spine and good water-line, arms at your sides, toes pointed. Drop the heel of your right foot down about twelve inches into the water. Force it up quickly and create a visible boil. Try it with your left foot. Now try it

Figure 29a Pushing Water up   **Figure 29b ⊘ Pushing Water Down**

alternating feet. As the one foot forces the water up, the heel of the other foot drops down.

Step 5: Kick at a tempo that there is no distinction on the surface of the water between the boil from one foot and that of the other. Continue to the other end of the pool, using a more forceful upward motion, and a gentler downward motion. Repeat for several lengths, feeling the difference between the water on your foot as you force it upwards, and as you drop your heel down.

DRILL FEEDBACK CHART

Problem	Modification
I can't make the water boil.	Try relaxing your foot and ankle, so that your foot works more like the tail of a fish. See the Floppy Foot drill to work on this.
My toes keep breaking the surface.	Point your toes more. Control your kick so your feet remain connected to the water.
I am not moving.	Remember to kick with more force upward than downward. Check that your toes are pointed, and that your knees are not bending too much.

No Knees Streamline Kick

30

THE PURPOSE OF THIS DRILL
- Learning to keep the knees under the water
- Using the correct muscles to kick backstroke
- Developing an efficient backstroke kick

HOW TO DO THIS DRILL

Step 1: Lay horizontally in the water, face up, straight spine and good water-line, toes pointed. Extend your arms over your head, squeezing your ears between your elbows and clasping your hands, one over the other. Begin the flutter kick, kicking upward with more force.

Step 2: Kick at a tempo that there is no distinction on the surface of the water between the boil from one foot and the other. Maintaining a neutral chin position, use your peripheral vision to see if your knees are breaking the surface of the water, or if the water is moving upward around your knees. If so, this indicates that you are lifting your knees, or doing a

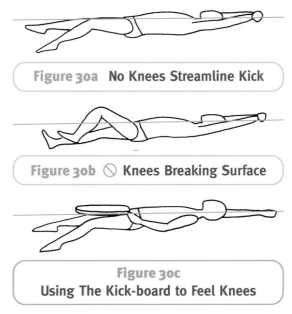

Figure 30a No Knees Streamline Kick

Figure 30b ⃠ Knees Breaking Surface

Figure 30c
Using The Kick-board to Feel Knees

bicycling motion during your kick. This is common because the muscles used to lift the knees, the abductors, that connect the legs to the abdomen, are used a great deal by humans on land in actions such as walking, running, cycling and climbing stairs. However, in the backstroke kick, lifting your knees weakens your kick.

Step 3: To engage the correct backstroke kicking muscles, the quads and the hamstrings, resume your backstroke float, hands leading, spine straight, good water-line, squeezing your ears with your elbows, and begin kicking with absolutely no bend at the hips. It means you have to start the kick lower than the surface of the water, and use your leg as if to kick a ball floating on the surface of the water. Although your knee will bend, it is only as a result of your dropping your heel into the water, not by lifting your knee. Imagine kicking a ball with your foot by raising your knee. It wouldn't work. Using your peripheral vision, check your knees. There should be no water moving around them. Practice for several lengths of the pool.

Step 4: Now, double check if you are lifting your knees by holding a kickboard with one hand, positioning it the long way over your upper legs and knees as you float and kick, keeping the other arm extended over your head. As you kick, you will be able to feel if your knees bump the kickboard. Practice for several lengths of the pool.

DRILL FEEDBACK CHART

Problem	Modification
Water gets in my face . . . a lot.	This is feedback that you are lifting your knees. Doing so produces a wave, which washes over your face. Work on starting the kick by dropping your heel down, rather than raising your knee up. Try it on land looking in a mirror. Also, in the water try kicking faster to produce more forward momentum.
It hurts my lower back when I don't bend my knees.	Rotate your pelvis forward and work on your straight spine using the Float on Your Spine drill. You also might be kicking too deep. The backstroke kick is only about twelve inches at its deepest. Additionally, make sure you are not kicking down with force. Simply drop your heel into the water. Kick with force only in the upward direction.
I move very well even with my knees breaking the surface.	You are probably blessed with excellent ankle flexibility which makes the backstroke kick much easier. But just think how well you would move if you also eliminated the drag that your knees are producing. It is worth your time to work on this.

Pigeontoed Kicking

THE PURPOSE OF THIS DRILL
- Feeling the most advantageous foot position
- Using the most foot surface to kick
- Developing a centralized kick

HOW TO DO THIS DRILL

Step 1: Lay on your back in the water. Achieve a straight spine, good water-line, and pointed toes. Extend your arms over your head, squeezing your ears between your elbows and clasping your hands, one over the other. Begin the flutter kick.

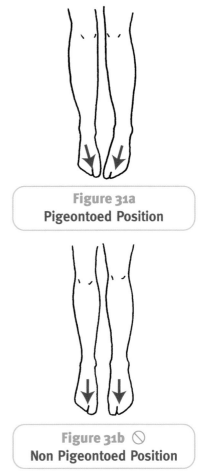

Figure 31a
Pigeontoed Position

Step 2: Point your toes and use a quick kick tempo. Kick upward with more force, creating a boil on the surface of the water. Notice that the part of your foot that comes closest to the surface is your big toe. Kick to the far end of the pool.

Step 3: Now push off the wall again for the backstroke kick. This time, turn your feet inward to the pigeontoed position, so your big toes are closer together than the rest of your feet. Notice that by turning your feet inward, your knees and hips are also internally rotated. Begin kicking.

Figure 31b ⃠
Non Pigeontoed Position

Step 4: Continue kicking with a quick tempo. Feel the top of your foot press upward against the water. Notice that you are engaging more of your foot's surface by positioning your pigeontoed feet. Notice too that your kick is more productive. Kick to the far end of the pool.

Step 5: Push off again for the backstroke kick. Achieve the pigeontoed position and kick at a quick tempo. Kick the water upward. Notice the centralized boil on the surface of the water. Notice too that your knees stay under the surface of the water better. Continue kicking for several lengths of the pool.

100

DRILL FEEDBACK CHART

Problem	Modification
My big toes bump into each other.	An occasional bump is okay. If your big toes are bumping into each other with every kick, this could slow your kick rhythm. Adjust the pitch of your feet very slightly so they don't touch.
My feet don't rotate this way.	Try it on land first. Turn your knees inward and let your feet follow. You can increase your flexibility by practicing it over time.
I still feel the downbeat more.	Engage your quads to kick upward. Try not to use your hamstrings to an equal extent. Drop your heel down, then force the top of your foot up quickly for the most effective backstroke kicking action.

32 Quarter Roll with Cup on Forehead

THE PURPOSE OF THIS DRILL
- Developing a balanced, effective kick
- Understanding the changing orientation of the kick
- Maintaining a stable head position while kicking

HOW TO DO THIS DRILL
Step 1: Fill a medium plastic cup halfway with water. Gently balance the cup on your forehead as you lay on your back in the water, with a straight spine and good water-line. Once the cup is balanced, position both arms at your sides. Begin kicking, toes pointed, knees underwater, making the water boil. Continue kicking to the other end of the pool, trying to keep the cup of water balanced on your forehead. If it falls off, stand and start again. Practice until you can kick productively without the cup falling off for a full length of the pool.

Step 2: Now prepare to kick another length with the cup on your forehead. This time, every six kicks, do a quarter roll. Keeping your head still so the cup remains balanced, roll your body clockwise, so that your left shoulder, arm and hip are out of the water, while your right shoulder, arm and hip are low in the water. Your kick should now be oriented to the side.

Step 3: After six kicks, roll your body a quarter turn counter-clockwise, so you are again flat on your back,

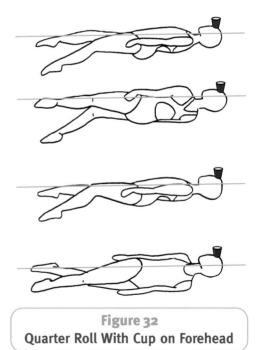

Figure 32
Quarter Roll With Cup on Forehead

and your kick is up and down. Do six kicks. Now, maintaining your head position so the cup stays on your forehead, turn your body a quarter turn clockwise again, so that your right shoulder, arm and hip are out of the water, while your left shoulder, arm and hip are low in the water. After six kicks, roll back to the flat back floating position, kicking up and down.

Step 4: Continue kicking with quarter rolls to the end of the pool, with your head still so that the cup remains balanced on your forehead. If the cup falls off, start again. This is not an easy drill! Practice until you can kick productively, with quarter rolls, while the cup remains on your forehead for several lengths of the pool.

DRILL FEEDBACK CHART

Problem	Modification
The cup falls off right away, even without a quarter roll.	Work on your straight spine and neutral chin. Work on the drills in the section called Body Position. Make sure your ears are underwater and your neck is relaxed.
When I do a quarter roll, my head turns too, and the cup falls off.	Relax your neck and turn your shoulder toward your cheek. Try it on land first, looking in a mirror.
My kick still aims up even with a quarter roll to the left or right.	Use more core stability, so that your shoulders and hips roll together and don't twist at the waist, leaving your hips flat.

103

ARM STROKE DRILLS

Of the many misconceptions about the backstroke arm stroke, the most common is that the arms remain straight throughout the stroke, like a windmill. A straight arm stroke is often associated with shoulder problems. It is also difficult, like trying to lift yourself out of the pool with straight arms. While it is important to begin and finish the stroke with straight, well aligned arms, using a high and firm bent elbow position, during the middle of the stroke, allows the swimmer to access more power, and move forward with an accelerating pull then push action. The goal of the following arm stroke drills for backstroke is to learn the most productive path of the underwater stroke for an easier, more effective, shoulder-saving stroke.

33 One Arm Pull/Push

THE PURPOSE OF THIS DRILL
- Learning the path of the backstroke arms
- Feeling both pull and push
- Rolling into and out of each stroke

HOW TO DO THIS DRILL
Step 1: Float in the water, face up, spine straight, good water-line, kicking productively, with one arm at your side and the other extended over your head, aligned with the shoulder.

Step 2: Start your stroke by descending your reaching hand about twelve inches straight down into the water, pinkie finger first, allowing the opposite shoulder and hip to rise at the same time. From twelve inches deep, keeping your elbow absolutely still, begin to move your fingertips and palm upward to press the water toward your feet. Sweep your hand to the height of your shoulder, so that your arm is close to a right angle. Done correctly, it should feel like your forearm is rotating around your elbow. This is the pull portion of the backstroke arms.

Step 3: From that point, straighten your arm in a quick sweep until your hand stops below your hip, with your fingertips pointing toward your feet. Allow your whole arm to become involved

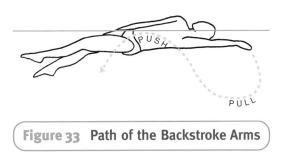

Figure 33 **Path of the Backstroke Arms**

in this sweep. At the same time, roll your same side hip upward to assist in the power of this action. This is the push portion of the backstroke arms.

Step 4: Recover your arm over the water and repeat the path of the backstroke arm with the same arm. Notice that your hand is tracing a sort of "S" shape along the side of your body. The top curve is the pull, the bottom curve is the push. This "S" shape can become more pronounced as you increase your roll into the top curve with your shoulder and hip, and out of the bottom curve with your shoulder and hip. Continue to the end of the pool.

Step 5: Repeat the drill, quickening your tempo, and accelerating your hand toward your hip. Hold your elbow firm. Roll in and roll out of each stroke. Try to identify the transition between pull and push. Continue for several lengths, then switch arms.

DRILL FEEDBACK CHART

Problem	Modification
It hurts my shoulder to get my hand twelve inches deep at the beginning of the stroke.	It is very important to allow your same side shoulder and hip to roll down with your hand. Without this roll, it is nearly impossible, and painful for many swimmers, as the shoulder joint is not designed for this range of motion from a flat position.
The palm of my hand is facing up when my hand reaches my hip.	This indicates that the path of your stroke is circular, instead of "S" shaped. When you finish with your palm up, you are lifting the water. Doing so actually pulls your body down, not forward. Try tracing the shape of an "S" in the air, then again in the water.
My fingertips come out of the water when my hand and shoulder line up.	Your hand might be too close to your shoulder. Keep it at a right angle to your shoulder. Also, be sure that you are rolling into your stroke with your shoulder and hip, giving you water over your fingertips when you your fingertips are closest to the water's surface.

Up and Over

THE PURPOSE OF THIS DRILL
- Feeling the path of the backstroke arms
- Maintaining a stable elbow position
- Catching deep water

HOW TO DO THIS DRILL

Step 1: Push off the wall for the backstroke, both arms extended over your head. Achieve a straight spine, firm core and good water-line. Establish a productive kick. Begin the backstroke arm stroke with your right arm, leaving your left arm in the extended position.

Step 2: Lower your right hand about twelve inches down into the water by rolling the same side shoulder and hip down, and the opposite shoulder and hip up. As your hand reaches its deepest point, catch a handful of water. Maintaining a stable elbow position, move your handful of water in an arch up and over your elbow.

Step 3: At the highest point in the arch, your fingers should be pointing upward toward the surface of the water, but not breaking the surface. At the finish of the arch, your arm should be straight along the side of your body, and your fingertips should be pointing toward your feet.

Step 4: As your right arm exits the water by your hip and returns over the water to its starting position, trace the same path with your left arm. Roll your left hip and shoulder down into the water, causing your left hand to come to a depth of about twelve inches. Grab hold of deep water, and sweep your hand up and over your still elbow in an arch that finishes with your arm straight at your side.

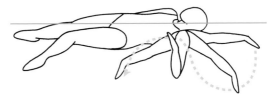

Figure 34 **Hands Travels Up and Over Past Shoulder**

Step 5: Continue stroking with alternating arms. Catch the water deep and keep hold it as your hand traces an arch up and over your elbow with each stroke. Trace the arch with more speed. Feel your body move forward with each stroke. Practice for several lengths of the pool.

DRILL FEEDBACK CHART

Problem	Modification
My hand breaks the surface at the top of the arch.	This indicates you are too flat in the water. Make sure you roll your body with your descending arm to get the depth you need at the top of the arch.
I can't seem to catch the water.	As your hand reaches its deepest point, move your fingertips and hand upward into position to press against the water. Keep your elbow firm and still at this point.
I lose my handful of water at the end of the arch.	Accelerate your motion through the arch. Your hand should be moving fastest at the end of the arch, pressing the water down and past your hip.

Fist Backstroke

THE PURPOSE OF THIS DRILL
* Learning to feel the water with the forearm
* Using a stable, high elbow
* Appreciating the role of the hand

HOW TO DO THIS DRILL
Step 1: Push off the wall for the backstroke. Before the first stroke, form closed fists with each hand.

Step 2: Start to stroke. At first it may seem impossible to make forward progress without the paddle of your open hand. Keep stroking, purposely positioning your arm so your forearm works as your paddle to press against the water. This will require you to initiate the stroke by moving your fists without moving your elbows, and to keep your elbows high and stable as your fist moves past them.

Step 3: Use the whole length of the stroke, top to bottom. Feel pull and push. Accelerate the underwater stroke. Maintain opposition. Adapt your stroke to the handless paddle. Continue to the other end of the pool.

Step 4: Now push off again, this time with open hands. Swim regular backstroke, using your hand as well as your forearm to press against the water. Keep a stable, elbow high. Feel pull and push. Accelerate your stroke. Maintain opposition.

Step 5: Continue alternating lengths of fist and open hand until you are feeling the water with a paddle that includes both your hand and your forearm.

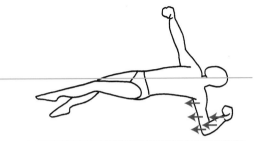

Figure 35 Fist Backstroke Using Arm Surface as Paddle

DRILL FEEDBACK CHART

Problem	Modification
I am not moving.	Reposition your forearm so when your arm moves through the stroke, it quickly becomes perpendicular to the surface of the water.
I am not feeling my forearm against the water.	Keep your elbow still as you move your fist, then move your forearm upward into position to press back on the water. If your elbow drops at this point, your forearm will not engage the water.
My elbows keep moving.	Try widening the angle of your bent arm through the beginning and middle of the underwater arm stroke. Move your fist before your forearm.

Corkscrew

36

THE PURPOSE OF THIS DRILL
* Achieving depth to begin the stroke
* Feeling the roll that begins the arm stroke
* Using a bent arm mid-pull similar to freestyle

HOW TO DO THIS DRILL
Step 1: Push off the wall for the backstroke with your arms extended. Achieve a straight spine and good water-line. Kick productively.

Step 2: Take one stroke with your left arm. As your left arm reaches your side, begin to stroke with your right arm while your left arm starts its recovery over the water.

Step 3: When your right arm approaches mid-recovery, your left arm should have come to its deepest point under-water. The shoulder and hip of your recovering arm should be at least partially out of the water, and the shoulder and hip of your stroking arm should be low in the water.

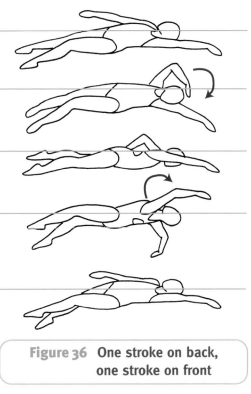

Step 4: At this point, redirect your recovery to cross over toward your opposite shoulder, and lead your body to switch from its side, to a front floating position. Your recovering hand should enter the water as a freestyle stroke.

Figure 36 One stroke on back, one stroke on front

111

Step 5: Start to stroke with freestyle as the arm at your side starts to recover as freestyle. You should again be floating on your side, and by mid-recovery, redirect your over-the-water-arm to enter the water as the backstroke.

Step 6: Continue to move through the water, one stroke as back-stroke and the next as freestyle. Feel the depth that your arm achieves to begin each stroke on your back. Notice the similar bent elbow position of your arms in both strokes during the mid-pull. Feel how rolling toward your stroking arm accesses more power for the stroke.

DRILL FEEDBACK CHART

Problem	Modification
I am getting dizzy.	Yes, this can happen. Stop frequently. Make the most of each stroke that you are able to do. Be very focused on noticing the depth that your hand achieves, the bent arm position in the middle of the stroke, and your roll until you feel dizzy.
It is hard to flip from my back to my front.	Allow your body to roll onto its side, using your hips and shoulders. Then simply continue that roll so you end up floating on your front.
I can't figure out when to breathe.	Catch a breath during the stroke on your back. This drill does not accommodate breathing during the freestyle stroke.

RECOVERY DRILLS

The opposition timing of the backstroke makes the arm stroke recovery an active part of the stroke. While resting the muscles of the arm, the recovering arm must serve as a counterbalance to the stroking arm. Accomplishing this requires the recovering arm to be aligned correctly itself in relation to the rest of the body. The following backstroke recovery drills focus on developing a relaxed, aligned and balanced path over the water.

Clock Arms

37

THE PURPOSE OF THIS DRILL
* Using an aligned entry position
* Learning to avoid over-reaching
* Feeling the natural range of motion of the shoulder

HOW TO DO THIS DRILL
Step 1: Stand in front of a full-length mirror. Imagine the face of a large clock centered on the mirror in front of you. Raise your right arm over your head as if preparing to enter the water for the backstroke, pinkie first. Position your hand at 12:00. Now, attempt to lower your arm downward as you would into the water to a point about twelve inches below where the water's surface would be. Notice that from the 12:00 position, your shoulder does not allow this rotation, unless you are double-jointed.

Step 2: Again, raise your right arm over your head extended as if preparing to enter the water for the backstroke. This time, position your arm at 1:00, and attempt to lower your arm as you would into the water to a point about twelve inches below where the water's surface would be. Notice that your shoulder allows this rotation, moving more freely around the joint. Some swimmers may need to use a 1:30 or 2:00 for a more comfortable entry point.

Step 3: Once you have found an entry point that allows free shoulder joint rotation, try duplicating this entry point with the other arm. Now try alternating arm action, monitoring your clock arms in the mirror in order to avoid an "over-reaching" 12:00 entry. Continue for 30 seconds.

Step 4: Now, try alternating arm action with your eyes closed. Every six or seven strokes, freeze at your entry position, open your eyes, and check if you are properly aligned at 1:00 or 11:00 so your arm can descend freely downward and you are aligned most directly forward. Once you have checked, and made a modification if necessary, resume your stroke action with your eyes closed. Check again. Continue until you are able to maintain a recovery with a well-aligned entry position.

Step 5: Now try it in the water. If you are swimming in an indoor pool, use the beams, pipes or lines on the ceiling to align your arms at 1:00 and 11:00. If you are swimming in an outdoor pool, keep imagining the clock around you, and align your arms outside 12:00. Practice lowering each arm down into the water to begin the stroke, and notice if your arm is rotating easily around the shoulder joint. Practice aligning your arm precisely in the direction you are heading. Continue until you are achieving a well-aligned entry that both allows your arm to achieve a wider range of motion and moves you most directly forward.

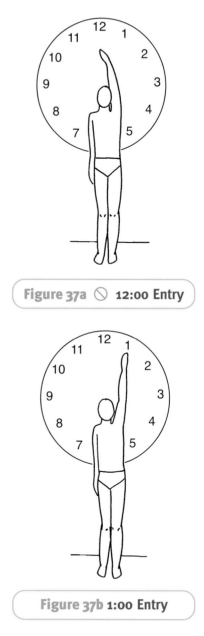

Figure 37a ⃠ **12:00 Entry**

Figure 37b 1:00 Entry

DRILL FEEDBACK CHART

Problem	Modification
I am comfortably able to enter the water at 12:00.	You are very fortunate to be so flexible. However, you still will want to strive for a 1:00 entry, so your whole body will be aligned forward, in the direction you are going.
When I think I am at 1:00, I am at 12:00.	This is true for most people. So, if you are trying to achieve a 1:00 entry, reach for 2:00.
My shoulder doesn't rotate freely even at 1:00.	Try reaching farther outside the shoulder. Also, remember to only lower your arm about twelve inches down into the water.

38 Two-step Recovery

THE PURPOSE OF THIS DRILL
- Establishing the path of the recovery
- Feeling correct recovery alignment
- Avoiding an over-reaching entry

HOW TO DO THIS DRILL

Step 1: Push off the wall preparing to do the backstroke, both arms extended over your head, straight spine, good water-line, productive kick.

Step 2: Take one stroke, leaving the other arm extended. When your arm finishes the underwater phase of the stroke past your hip, slide it straight out of the water, up-ward past the side of your body. Establish the path of your recovery by tracing a half-circle in the air, from the place where your arm exited the water to the point it will enter, extended past your shoulder, aligned in the direction you are heading. Repeat with the other arm, focusing on the forward-aimed, arched path of the recovering arm.

Step 3: Now, as your arm begins the recovery after the next stroke, begin to

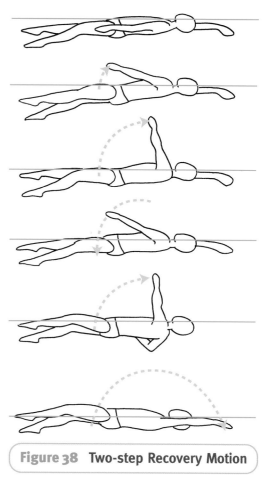

Figure 38 Two-step Recovery Motion

trace the arch over the water, but stop your arm at the highest point in the arch and count to five. Notice the alignment to your higher arm. It should be directly above your shoulder, pointing to the sky, not above your face. A misaligned recovery leads to an over-reaching entry that starts the stroke from a position of weakness.

Step 4: After the count of five, lower your arm back into the water, following the same recovery path in reverse, finishing with your hand past your hip. Count to five, and begin recovery again, this time tracing the whole recovery path and entering the water extended past your shoulder. Check your alignment at the high point as your arm passes. As your arm begins this second, full recovery, the extended arm begins its underwater stroke.

Step 5: When the second arm completes the underwater stroke, again do a half recovery, then the complete recover. Continue to the far end of the pool, alternating arms with a two-step recovery. Practice for several lengths until the path of the recovery is well aligned with your shoulder at the top of the arch, and not over-reaching to the center at entry.

DRILL FEEDBACK CHART

Problem	Modification
I sink when I hold my arm up in the middle of the recovery.	It is awkward at first. During the five seconds that your arm is at the top of the arch, kick harder. Focus on your straight spine and core stability.
My arm aligns with my face.	It is important to work on this because correct alignment begins the stroke from a position of strength. If your arm is over-reached during the recovery, you will enter the water with a shoulder position that does not allow the range of motion you need. You will then not be able to get your hand to the optimal depth to stroke in a high elbow position.
I have no momentum.	Your momentum is reduced because of the lack of opposition in this drill. Remember that the point of this drill is to work on your recovery alignment. Focus on that rather than how fast you are going.

Locked Elbow Drill

THE PURPOSE OF THIS DRILL
- Learning to fully align your recovering arm
- Extending the stroke range by locking the recovering elbow
- Feeling opposition balance

HOW TO DO THIS DRILL
Step 1: Holding a piece of chalk in your hand, stand with your back against a wall. Trace around the shape of your shoulders and head.

Step 2: Still standing within your chalk outline on the wall, extend the arm with the chalk, as if preparing to enter the water from your backstroke recovery. Make a mark on the wall in that position. Return your arm to your side.

Step 3: Again extend your chalk arm, but as you approach the entry position, push your elbow to the locked position, as if you would if trying to reach something on a shelf that is a bit too high. Make another mark on the wall, using more pressure in order to distinguish it from the first mark.

Step 4: Step away from the wall and compare the two marks. Notice that by locking your elbow, the second mark aligns above your shoulder, where as

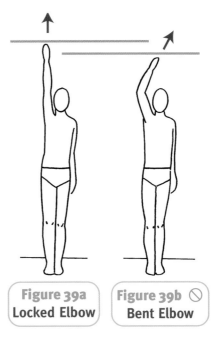

Figure 39a
Locked Elbow

Figure 39b ⃠
Bent Elbow

the first mark aligns more closely with your head. In addition, many swimmers will notice that simply locking their elbow, the second mark will be higher on the wall by several inches, indicating a longer stroke. Try it with the other arm.

Step 5: Now, get in the water and push off the wall for the backstroke, arms extended over your head, spine straight, good water-line, and productive kick. Take one underwater stroke ending past your hip. Begin your recovery focusing on your elbow. Look for any bend in your recovering arm at any point during the arching path over the water. Swim backstroke to the far end of the pool, watching each recovery, and checking for any bend in your elbow.

Step 6: Again swim regular backstroke. As each stroke ends past your hip, deliberately push your elbow to the locked position before starting the recovery. Maintain your locked elbow throughout the recovery. Notice that your stroke will feel longer. Notice too that your locked elbow recovering arm will feel more connected to the underwater arm, as it creates an opposition balance while they move in conjunction. Notice as well that you will be able to feel the water better as your recovery arm transitions to the stroking arm.

DRILL FEEDBACK CHART

Problem	Modification
I can't feel a locked elbow when I am swimming.	Try it on land until you develop the feeling. Use a mirror. Close your eyes and extend your arm over your head with what you think is a locked elbow. Then open your eyes to check. If it is not locked, make the correction while looking in the mirror. Try again with your eyes closed and re-check.
I can't see if my elbow remains locked when it enters the water.	This is true, but by achieving a locked elbow during recovery, you have a greater chance of maintaining that position through entry. Focus on the feeling at entry of reaching for something on a shelf that is a bit too high.
When I focus on my recovering arm, both arms end up at my sides.	Remember that beyond alignment, the main benefit of a locked elbow is that it increases the opposition balance, or feeling of connection between the arms. Both arms must move at the same time, on opposite sides of the body, and in opposing action. When one arm is at its highest, the other is at its lowest. When one arm is beginning the stroke, the other is finishing the stroke. Focus on this balance.

Dog-ears

4O

THE PURPOSE OF THIS DRILL
- Feeling an outward hand pitch
- Maintaining a firm arm and a relaxed hand
- Avoiding a collapsed wrist at entry

HOW TO DO THIS DRILL

Step 1: Push off the wall for the backstroke. Achieve a straight spine, good water-line, opposition balance, and locked recovering elbow. Kick productively. Stroke through and recover. After recovery, your hand should enter the water pinkie first, slicing the water, rather than making a hole in it with your flat hand. This requires positioning your hand with the palm facing outward. Try the palms out entry for several strokes.

Step 2: Now, swim backstroke again, maintaining a palms-out entry position at the end of recovery. Freeze in the position when your arm has passed the top of the recovery arch. Observe which way your fingers are pointing. If they are pointing inward toward your face, and you are seeing the back of your hand, you have a collapsed wrist. A collapsed wrist positions your palms upward, as if you were a waiter holding a tray over your shoulder. It is the weakest entry

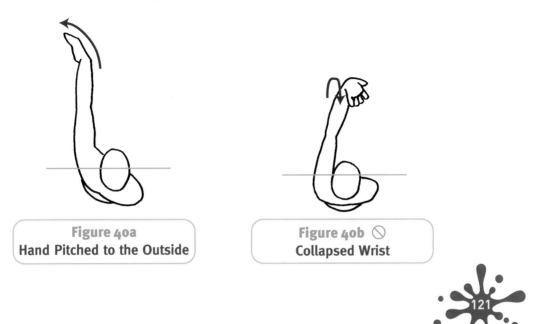

| Figure 40a | Figure 40b ⊘ |
| Hand Pitched to the Outside | Collapsed Wrist |

position possible, and a disruption in your alignment. Notice that with a collapsed wrist, the muscles in your forearms are working, rather than resting during recovery. Notice too, that with a collapsed wrist, it is much harder to maintain a locked elbow recovery. Continue swimming, avoiding a collapsed wrist.

Step 3: Now, with your locked elbow, palms-out recovering arm, deliberately allow that hand to flop to the outside at the wrist, relaxing your fingers as you do. This is the Dog-ears position. Notice that your forearm becomes more relaxed simply by changing your wrist position. Notice too that with your hand in an outwardly pitched position, when your hand lowers into the water, it is positioned perfectly to grab a handful of water.

Step 4: Continue swimming backstroke with a dog-eared recovery. Increase your stroke rate. Grab a handful of water with each entry, hold on to it, and move your body past your hand.

DRILL FEEDBACK CHART

Problem	Modification
My wrist isn't relaxed.	Try wiggling your fingers during your recovery, and flopping your hand back and forth as if it had no bones.
I can't see if my hand is still dog-eared at entry.	Try it on land until you develop the feeling. Use a mirror. Close your eyes, extend your arm over your head using what you think is a dog-eared hand. Then open your eyes to check. If it is not, make the correction while looking in the mirror. Take time to feel what muscles are involved. Try again with your eyes closed and re-check.
The back of my hand slaps the water in the dog-eared position.	Remember to first position your hand so that your pinkie enters the water first, and then add the dog-eared hand position.

BREATHING DRILLS

Without your face in the water, it would seem that breathing drills for backstroke are a low priority. The opposite is true. Because rhythmic breathing is an essential part of sustaining any swimming stroke, learning to develop a good breathing rhythm in the backstroke is a top priority. In addition, because the power of the backstroke kick is upward, against gravity, frequent oxygen exchange is required. Many swimmers dislike backstroke because water gets in their face. Learning to time the breathing to the rhythm of the waves of the stroke, makes the backstroke much more enjoyable. The goal of the following backstroke breathing drills is to develop rhythmic breathing and more a comfortable, productive backstroke.

41 Rhythmic Breathing Sequence

THE PURPOSE OF THIS DRILL
- Experimenting with different breathing rhythms
- Matching the stroke rate and the breathing rhythm
- Becoming comfortable breathing in the backstroke

HOW TO DO THIS DRILL

Step 1: Stand with your hand on your abdomen, between your breastbone and your belly button. Close your eyes and breathe normally. Feel the rhythm of your breathing as you inhale and exhale. Now, maintaining the same rhythm, breathe as if you were in the water, inhaling through your mouth and exhaling through both nose and mouth.

Step 2: Now, in the pool, push off the wall preparing to do the backstroke, spine straight, good water-line, productive kick, locked elbows, hands pitched out. Try to duplicate the breathing rhythm you did on land. Swim at a rate so that your inhale happens as one arm recovers, and your exhale happens when the other arm recovers. Continue for several lengths of the pool, resting at the end of each length.

Step 3: Next, try a quicker stroke rate. Match your breathing to your quicker stroke rate, in-

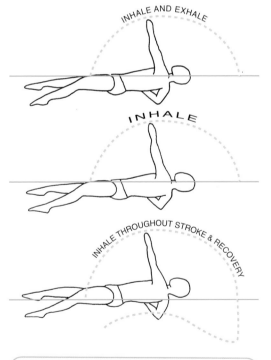

Figure 41 Three Breathing Rhythms for the Backstroke

haling on one arm, and exhaling on the other. Notice, that with a quicker stroke rate, this breathing rhythm doesn't work as well. There is not time to fully inhale or exhale. Change your breathing rhythm to inhale with one full stroke cycle (one stroke with each arm), and then exhale on the next stroke cycle. Notice that your breathing rhythm more closely resembles your "normal" breathing rhythm using this timing. Continue for several lengths of the pool, resting after each length.

Step 4: Now, try a stroke rate that is very relaxed and easy, perhaps resembling warm-up speed. Inhale with one stroke cycle, exhale with the next. Notice, that at this slower stroke rate, this breathing rhythm doesn't work as well. The exchange of air is not frequent enough. Change your breathing rhythm so you are both inhaling and exhaling with each arm recovery, doing the same thing on the next arm. Notice that the breathing rhythm is now more normal. Continue for several lengths of the pool, resting after each length.

DRILL FEEDBACK CHART

Problem	Modification
As I get tired, my breathing gets irregular.	Maintain a regular breathing rhythm as long as you can, then rest and try it again. As you practice more, you will be able to hold on to the rhythm for longer.
I can't maintain the rhythm when water gets in my face.	It is hard to get used to water washing over your face, but with practice, and increased momentum, you will notice a pattern to most of the splashes. This will help with your breathing timing (see the next drill).
When I go faster, I need more air, so I breathe more frequently.	If inhaling with one arm and exhaling with the other arm isn't frequent enough, try inhaling and exhaling with each arm. If that is not frequent enough, slow down your stroke rate, and try to make more forward progress with each stroke in order to go faster.

42 The Breathing Pocket

THE PURPOSE OF THIS DRILL
- Using the ebb and flow of the water to time your breathing
- Finding another benefit of the roll in and out of the stroke
- Becoming comfortable when breathing in the backstroke

HOW TO DO THIS DRILL
Step 1: Push off the wall preparing to do the backstroke, spine straight, good water-line, productive kick, locked elbow recovery, dog-eared hand. Focus on rolling into and out of each stroke, feeling opposition. Take several strokes, then freeze at the point that one

arm is in mid-stroke under-water, and the other arm is in mid-recovery. At this point, the armpit of your recovering arm should be completely out of the water, and the shoulder of the other arm should be at its lowest point under the water.

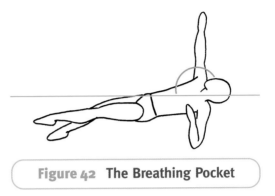

Figure 42 The Breathing Pocket

Step 2: Observe that in this position and point in the stroke, the raised armpit side forms a barrier to the water that would otherwise be in your face. Resume stroking. Notice that this barrier is only in place for a very brief moment. This is your breathing pocket. It is your chance to inhale without water going in your face.

Step 3: Swim backstroke again, exaggerating your roll to make the breathing pocket very clear. Try to find the breathing pocket on each side of your body. Continue swimming backstroke inhaling in your breathing pocket with each stroke.

DRILL FEEDBACK CHART

Problem	Modification
I still get water in my face.	Work on maintaining your spine straight and a good water-line. Make sure your kick is productive without any bicycling action. Try rolling more.
Water still goes over my face when I exhale.	That is fine. As long as you are exhaling through your nose and mouth, water won't go in.
I have a better breathing pocket on one side.	This indicates that you are rolling more on one side than the other. It would be best to work on developing a symmetrical roll so that you have equal breathing pockets, and have more choices in changing your breathing pattern.

LEVERAGE DRILLS

Leverage in the backstroke adds potential power to the stroke, increases the range of motion at the beginning of the stroke, and enables the swimmer to sustain the stroke longer. It is achieved similar to freestyle, through the side to side rolling action of a unified core. The goal of the following leverage drills for backstroke is to learn to incorporate a productive roll into the stroke.

Three Strokes Switch Backstroke

THE PURPOSE OF THIS DRILL
- Benefiting from core leverage
- Feeling the roll into and out of each stroke
- Transferring power from the core to the limbs

HOW TO DO THIS DRILL

Step 1: Push off the wall preparing to do the backstroke, straight spine and good water-line. Perform three strokes (one arm = one stroke), accompanied by a productive kick. As your arm approaches your hip on the third stroke, float and kick in that position, with the arm that just finished its underwater stroke at your side, the other arm fully extended. You should not be floating flat in the water, but instead you should be mostly on your side with the arm at your side closer to the surface, and the arm extended over your head lower in the

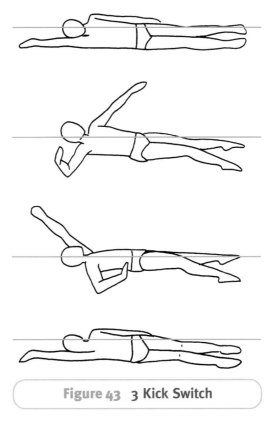

Figure 43   3 Kick Switch

water. Your face should remain out of the water the whole time. Do six good kicks in this position (one leg = one kick).

Step 2: With your sixth kick switch floating sides, by rolling toward the other hip and shoulder, but remaining face up. This roll should initiate three more strokes by bringing the high hip and shoulder down, and the low hip and shoulder up, while the arm at your side recovers over the water to the front, and the reaching arm begins its underwater stroke. Keep a steady kick through the whole process.

Step 3: Continue doing three strokes, kicking the whole time, and then six kicks in the side position until you reach the far end of the pool. Notice that your "switch" affects both arms at the same time.

Step 4: Repeat the drill, this time using three strokes and three kicks. As you become more comfortable, try to incorporate the switch between each stroke. Continue to the far end of the pool.

Step 5: Once you are able to roll productively with each stroke, begin swimming regular backstroke rolling into and out of each stroke, as you did in the drill. Practice for several length of the pool.

DRILL FEEDBACK CHART

Problem	Modification
I go crooked.	Be sure your leading arm is aligned at 1:00. You can swim next to a lane line, or if you are at an indoor pool, watch the lines on the ceiling to go straight.
I don't roll as much in the three strokes as I do changing to the kick only phase.	Slow down your strokes. Allow time to roll. Use both hips and shoulders to roll.
I am struggling to keep my face up during the kick only phase.	Try using a quicker kick rhythm. Kick up towards the surface with more force. It is important to maintain your momentum during the kick only phase.

One Arm Rope Climb

44

THE PURPOSE OF THIS DRILL
* Learning to anchor your reaching arm
* Feeling the high elbow position of strength
* Experiencing your body moving past your hand

HOW TO DO THIS DRILL
Step 1: String a rope from one end of the pool to the other, attaching it securely to the lane rope hooks in the side of the pool. The rope should be fairly tight, floating just below the surface of the water.

Step 2: Lay in the water on your back, one arm extended over your head, spine straight, good water-line, the rope just outside your extended arm. Grasp the rope with the hand of your extended arm. From this anchor point, pull your body past your hand, with a totally straight arm, moving your arm across the surface of the water, until the hand holding the rope is by your hip. Notice that as you move forward, no matter how much core stability you have, your legs swing toward the rope. Notice as well, that your shoulder is doing all the work.

Step 3: Grasp the rope again with your arm extended over your head. This time, drop your elbow down, lowering it into your ribs as you attempt to move your body past your anchored hand. Notice that it is very difficult to move your body forward with your elbow low and moving.

Step 4: Again, grasp the rope with your arm extended over your head. This time, pull your body up so that your shoulder is at the same level as your hand. Allow your elbow to bend

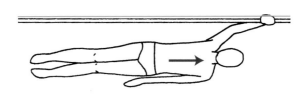

Figure 44 **Moving Body Past Anchored Hand**

up to a right angle, but remain about parallel to your shoulder and hand. From this point, straighten your arm. Keep your elbow firm as your body moves past your anchored hand. Notice that by keeping your elbow firm you have more leverage to move yourself forward. It is also easier and more productive than the other two ways that you tried.

Step 5: Continue the one arm rope climb using a high, stable elbow, and an accelerating arm action. When you reach the far end of the pool, switch arms. Practice several times with each arm. Once you

are able to clearly feel yourself move past your anchored hand, begin swimming regular back-stroke, anchoring your hand in the water, and again move your body past that point with each stroke.

DRILL FEEDBACK CHART

Problem	Modification
I end up under the rope.	Align the hand grabbing the rope with outside of your shoulder, and keep it outside of your shoulder the entire time.
It puts strain on my shoulder to pull with my arm straight.	Exactly. This part of the drill is designed as a contrast to doing the arm stroke correctly. It shows that the straight arm pull over-taxes the shoulder, where as the high elbow bent arm stroke allows you to stroke comfortably without pain.
I am not producing a glide.	Make sure your elbow in positioned high from the start. Move your body past your hand and elbow. Accelerate through to the end of the stroke.

Opposition Freeze Frame

THE PURPOSE OF THIS DRILL
* Understanding the role of opposition in backstroke leverage
* Checking opposition at various stages in the stroke
* Learning to maintain opposition

HOW TO DO THIS DRILL

Step 1: Push off the wall on your back, with both arms at your sides. Kick productively. With your right arm, do one complete backstroke, bringing your arm over the water in a fully aligned arch, then stroking through to your hip. When your right arm returns to its starting point, do the same thing with your left arm. Continue for twelve strokes. Notice that the forward motion you produce is not continuous, so that when your left arm is at your side and your right arm is in the air recovering, nothing is moving you forward except your kick. Notice too that it is difficult to roll into and out of your stroke, accessing core leverage. This is an example of backstroke without "opposition".

Step 2: Now, push off the wall with both arms extended over your head, preparing to do the backstroke, spine straight, good water-line, productive kick, locked elbows, hands pitched out. Establish opposition by doing an underwater stroke with one arm, while the other remains over your head. Roll toward the side of your body with the arm extended, so that side of your body becomes lower in the water. Now, begin swimming backstroke, focusing on maintaining opposition.

Step 3: Swim six strokes at a good strong pace. On the next stroke, freeze when your right hand has entered the water. Notice where your left hand is. It should be at the opposite extreme of the stroke, exiting the water past your hip.

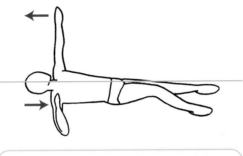

Figure 45 **Arm Stroke Opposition**

Step 4: Continue swimming backstroke. After six strokes, freeze again as your right hand transitions from pull to push. Notice where your left hand is. It should be opposite, in the middle of the recovery.

Step 5: Continue swimming backstroke. After each six strokes, freeze at a different point in the stroke, checking your opposition.

DRILL FEEDBACK CHART

Problem	Modification
My arms don't stay opposite.	Focus on the position with one arm extended over your head, and the other arm at your side. Use that as your home base. Find that position between each stroke, before starting the next one.
I don't have opposition in the middle of the stroke.	It might be that you are swimming too flat. In the middle of the stroke, you should be transitioning from pull to push with one arm, and passing the high point in the arch of the recovery with the other arm. The recovering side should be higher in the water than the side with underwater arm
If I don't bring both arms down when I push off, I can't get my face out of the water.	Use a quicker kick to get you most of the way to the surface, then stroke strongly with one arm to get into a swimming position with your face up. Practice this. It is very important.

Armpit Lift

THE PURPOSE OF THIS DRILL
- Balancing the recovery arm with the stroking arm
- Using core leverage
- Developing a unified stroke

HOW TO DO THIS DRILL
Step 1: Push off the wall preparing to do the backstroke, straight spine, good water-line, productive kick. Establish opposition. Roll into and out of each stroke.

Step 2: As your recovering arm approaches the top of the arch over the water, lift your armpit out of the water by rolling your opposite shoulder down lower into the water. Keep your elbow locked, and your hand aligned above your shoulder. When your recovering arm approaches the entry point beyond your shoulder, allow your armpit to submerge again.

Step 3: Recover with the other arm. Notice that when you lift the armpit at the top of the recovery arch, it affects the underwater stroking arm. Correctly balanced, lifting your armpit helps your other arm to transition from the pull phase to the push phase of the stroke, and, to produce important arm speed at the finish of the stroke.

Step 4: Continue stroking, and with each recovery, lift your armpit out of the water during the highest part of the arch. Continue for

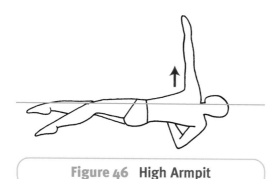

several lengths of the pool until you feel that the action of lifting your armpit balances the actions of the stroking arm. It should feel that the arms are working together, yet opposite.

Figure 46 High Armpit

DRILL FEEDBACK CHART

Problem	Modification
I sink when I lift my armpit.	It sounds like your arms are not balancing each other. When you are lifting the armpit of your recovering arm, the other arm should be bent at the elbow at approximately a right angle, your elbow high and stable. That hand should be gaining speed and beginning to push towards your feet. In any other relationship to each other, your stroke will not benefit from the armpit lift.
My feet fish-tail.	It is important for your recovering arm to remain aligned with its exit point and same side shoulder. Avoid entering the water with your hand at 12:00. Over-reaching like this will disrupt your alignment, causing you to fish-tail.
This seems to make my stroke pause.	Think of it as a transition instead of a pause. Both the recovering arm and underwater arm are moving at the point of the armpit lift. There should be no pause, just a feeling the arms are balancing each other and unified in their action.

COORDINATION DRILLS

Coordinated backstroke unifies the individual actions of the stroke into a seamless effort forward. With each part working together, the backstroke becomes easier, smoother, and more comfortable, as well as more productive. The goal of the following coordination drills is to bring together the many elements that contribute to a good backstroke and to use them in combination for efficient backstroke action.

Roll, Pull, Roll, Push

THE PURPOSE OF THIS DRILL
- Blending the actions of the roll and the arm stroke
- Initiating the arm stroke from the core
- Coordinating backstroke action

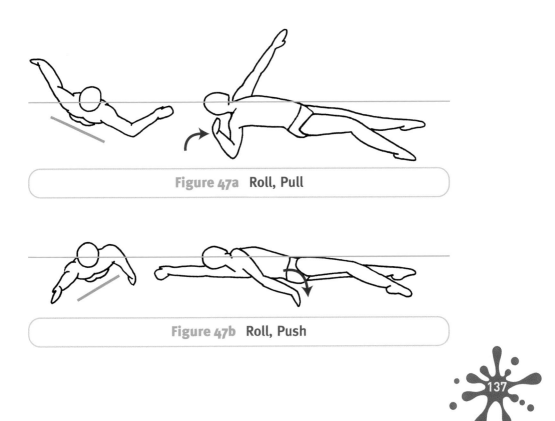

Figure 47a   **Roll, Pull**

Figure 47b   **Roll, Push**

HOW TO DO THIS DRILL

Step 1: Push off the wall on your back, both arms extended, preparing to do the backstroke, straight spine, good water-line, productive kick. Swim to the other end of the pool focusing on identifying the pull phase and the push phase in your backstroke arm stroke.

Step 2: Swim another length of backstroke, this time focusing on identifying the roll or "switch" from one side of your body to the other.

Step 3: Now, swim a length of backstroke timing the pull phase of the underwater arm stroke to begin as you "switch" toward the underwater arm. Then, with the same arm, time the push phase of the stroke to begin as you "switch" away from the underwater arm.

Step 4: Swim several lengths of the pool, focusing on the timing of roll, pull, roll push. Concentrate on one arm at a time. Once coordinated with the first arm, concentrate on the other arm to see if your timing also follows roll, pull, roll push.

Step 5: Practice until you can increase your stroke rate and still maintain this timing. This is the ideal backstroke coordination.

DRILL FEEDBACK CHART

Problem	Modification
This timing helps my pull but not my push.	Be sure you are switching with your hips as well as your shoulders in a unified action. Without your hips rolling too, your push will not benefit.
This timing helps my push, but not my pull.	Be sure your recovering arm is aligned with your shoulder so it has the range of motion to descend twelve inches into the water at entry with the roll. Without this depth, the pull will not be of benefit.
I lose the timing when I increase my stroke rate.	Think of it as a transition, instead of a pause. Both the recovering arm and underwater arm are moving at the point of the armpit lift. There should be no pause, just a feeling the arms are balancing each other and unified in their action.

Pinkie Lead

THE PURPOSE OF THIS DRILL
- Using the hip roll to initiate the recovery
- Eliminating extraneous actions
- Learning to avoid shoulder pain

HOW TO DO THIS DRILL

Step 1: Push off the wall on your back, both arms extended, preparing to do the backstroke, straight spine, good water-line, productive kick. Swim backstroke to the other end of the pool focusing on your hand at the end of the push phase of the arm stroke, just before recovery. Notice that your thumb is closest to your body as it finishes the push, and the pinkie is to the outside. In this position it is the back of the hand that exits first for recovery, creating a large hole in the water, and lifting heavy water upward into the recovery.

Step 2: To avoid this, traditionally, most swimmers have been taught to flip their hand to a thumb up position to exit the water, then flip their hand again during recovery to achieve a pinkie first entry at the end of recovery. Although the thumb-lead position avoids more drag than exiting with the back of your hand, it requires the additional action of flipping your hand over and then back again. This action is done independently from the roll, making the arm work harder. In addition, if not done early enough in the recovery, the second hand flip can contribute to shoulder pain. Practice the thumb-first recovery, initiating the flip to pinkie leading before your hand reaches the top of the recovery arch.

Step 3: The alternative to flipping your hand, before and again during recovery, is to allow your roll to position your hand for recovery. Swim back-

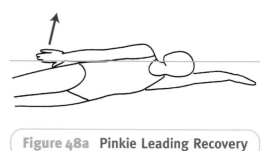

Figure 48a Pinkie Leading Recovery

stroke to the other end of the pool, feeling core stability that unites your shoulders and hips. Focus on your shoulder of the arm that is finishing the push phase of the underwater stroke. As the hand finishes the push, deliberately pop the same side shoulder out of the water just as your hand passes your hip. Notice that as you do this deliberate movement with your shoulder, your same hip will also rise. Practice to the far end of the pool.

Step 4: Now, swim another length of backstroke, focusing on popping your shoulder out of the water, and allowing your same side hip to rise at the point when your same side your hand is finishing the push. Freeze in that position. Observe that having rolled, it is the pinkie that is positioned to exit the water first for recovery. With the pinkie leading the recovery from start to finish, there is no need to flip the hand over and back, or to make sure the second flip is done early in the recovery to avoid shoulder pain.

Step 5: Repeat this drill, maintaining unified hip and shoulder action. With each stroke, deliberately pop your shoulder out of the water as your hand finishes the push. Feel your hip rise as your hand is finishing its push. Then, as the hip continues its switch, let it lift your hand out of the water in the same position the hand finished the push, pinkie leading. It is just less work than a thumb-lead recovery.

141

DRILL FEEDBACK CHART

Problem	Modification
To accomplish a pinkie leading recovery, I have to roll more.	Exactly. Maximize the benefit of your roll. Let it do the work of lifting your hand out of the water. Rest all you can during recovery.
With the pinkie leading, the recovery seems to be opposite to the way I was taught.	Yes, most of the teaching theory for swimming is based on using a flatter stroke, which depends more on arm and leg power alone. Incorporating leverage from the core changes the dynamics of swimming in many ways, including the under-recognized opportunity to let your roll action position your hand for recovery, pinkie leading.
So, a thumb-first recovery is fine as long as I flip my hand over early in recovery.	It is a widely accepted practice to exit thumbs-first. However, flipping your hand early in the recovery is worth trying, if only as a preventive measure to avoid shoulder pain that affects many backstrokers.

49 Backstroke Balance Drill with Cup

THE PURPOSE OF THIS DRILL
- Developing a balanced, effective backstroke
- Developing continuous backstroke motion
- Maintaining a stable head position while swimming backstroke

HOW TO DO THIS DRILL
Step 1: Fill a medium plastic cup half-way with water. Gently balance the cup on your forehead as you lay horizontally in the water, face

up, straight spine and good water-line. Once the cup is balanced, position both arms extended over your head. Kick productively.

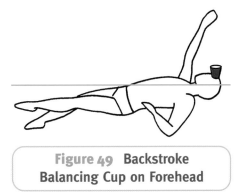

Step 2: Begin the underwater stroke with one arm, rolling smoothly into the stroke, while your head stays still, centered and neutral. Keep

Figure 49 Backstroke Balancing Cup on Forehead

the cup of water balanced on your forehead. When the first arm passes your hip, begin stroking with the other arm. If the cup falls off, stand and start again.

Step 3: Practice until you can swim smoothly for several strokes without the cup falling off your forehead.

Step 4: Swim backstroke again, with the cup on your forehead, increasing your stroke and kick rate, and maintaining your stable, neutral head position. Roll smoothly from side to side, and with your hips and shoulders united, While they are opposite, feel the movement of both of your arms initiated at once by a single action of the core. This is ultimate backstroke.

DRILL FEEDBACK CHART

Problem	Modification
The cup falls off right away.	Work on relaxing your neck muscles, so your head does not move with your shoulders. It should feel like your head is separate, floating ahead of your body.
The cup falls off when my hand enters the water.	Be sure you are not doing a wide kick at this point to help your arm enter the water with speed. You also might be entering the water with the back of your hand, which makes a big splash, rather than slicing the water smoothly by entering pinkie-first.
The cup falls off when I am recovering.	If your recovery is aligned over your face, it will drop water onto the cup on your forehead, knocking it off. Practice aligning your recovery over your shoulder, and aiming for a 1:00 entry.

Opposition Overlap

THE PURPOSE OF THIS DRILL
* Recognizing the momentary non-opposition point in the backstroke
* Making the most of both arms pressing on the water at once
* Feeling a continuous stroke

HOW TO DO THIS DRILL
Step 1: Push off the wall for backstroke, achieving a straight spine, good water-line, and productive kick. Swim backstroke to the other end of the pool. Focus on the opposition of the arm stroke. When one arm is under the water, one arm is over the water. When one arm is in mid-stroke under the water, the other arm is in mid-recovery.

Step 2: Now focus on the point when one arm is starting the stroke, and the other arm is finishing the stroke. This sounds opposite. As you swim, feel what is really happening. As one arm is entering the water and

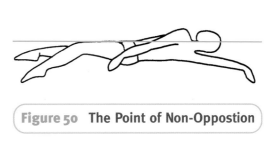

Figure 50   **The Point of Non-Oppostion**

descending about twelve inches downward, the other arm is still pushing past the hip. Both arms are in the water at the same time. Both are in the power phase of the stroke at the same time. For a moment, the arms are actually not opposite.

Step 3: Continue swimming backstroke, feeling this moment of overlap. Feel how the roll of the stroke assists both arms, one to start the arm stroke, the other to finish the arm stroke. Use this moment to start your stroke with power, and to finish your stroke with power. Practice more until you can feel both arms engaged in the power phase of the stroke at the same time, at opposite ends of the stroke.

Step 4: Kick to assist both the beginning and the end of the stroke. Feel the balance of the stroke shift from the finishing arm to the starting arm. Opposition is reset as the beginning arm sweeps into its anchored position at the same time as the other arm clears the water. Practice for several lengths of the pool. Develop a continuous stroke, using the moment of stroke overlap to access more power than with one arm at a time.

DRILL FEEDBACK CHART

Problem	Modification
I don't feel the overlap.	Make sure your entry hand is descending down into the water, and not stroking from the surface of the water. Also, make sure you are finishing the stroke by pushing all the way past your hip. The overlap happens when these two actions occur simultaneously.
I am flat at this point.	Make sure your arms are in continuous motion, and not stopped, one extended and one at your side. You should be in transition, rolling toward the side with the arm entering, and away from the side with the arm finishing. Practice this transition to make more use of leverage from your core.
My finishing arm is already at my side.	Stroke past the hip instead of into the hip. This will give you a longer stroke, establish the overlap, and create a continuous stroke.

DRILLS FOR
BREASTSTROKE

BODY POSITION DRILLS

Because drag is an inherent part of the breaststroke, achieving excellent body position is essential in maximizing the forward motion of the stroke. Like freestyle and backstroke, the core is the center of power, but in breaststroke, there is no side-to-side roll, instead, there is a tipping or rocking type motion. Achieving an effective rocking motion requires the swimmer to maintain a stable hip position, while the head and legs switch back and forth between the extremes of the tipping float. The goal of the following drills for breaststroke body position is to learn to use core tension to achieve the best floating technique, while minimizing drag and maximizing glide productivity.

Streamline

51

THE PURPOSE OF THIS DRILL
* Eliminating drag
* Achieving an advantageous breaststroke glide position
* Feeling effective core tension and stability

HOW TO DO THIS DRILL
Step 1: Position your feet wide apart on the wall and push off on your front still with your legs apart, arms extended but with your hands about thirty-six inches apart. You should be floating like an "X". With your face in the water, look forward. Float until you stop. Notice the distance you travelled.

Step 2: Again push off the wall in the same "X" position, put this time, lower your chin and look at the bottom of the pool. Float until you stop. Notice that the distance you travelled is farther. Simply by eliminating the frontal resistance of your face being forward, you bump into less water, and move forward better.

Step 3: Now push off the wall, with your legs apart, looking at the bottom of the pool, and this time clasp one hand over the other, and straighten your elbows so you are squeezing your ears between your arms. Your arms should be pointing forward, like an arrow. Float until you stop. Notice that the distance you travelled is even farther. By narrowing your leading edge, you bump into less water, moving forward better.

Step 4: Now push off the wall, looking at the bottom of the pool, clasping one hand over the other, with straight elbows, squeezing your ears between your arms. This time position your legs closer for the push off, then when you leave the wall hold them together, thigh to ankle. Float until you stop. Notice that the distance you travelled is much farther. By reducing the total space you take up, you bump into less water, and move forward better.

Step 5: Now push off the wall, looking at the bottom of the pool, clasping one hand over the other, with straight elbows, squeezing your ears between your arms, legs together, thigh to ankle. Engage

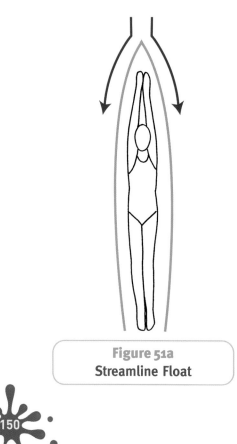

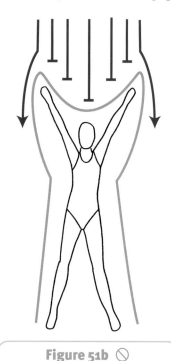

Figure 51a	Figure 51b ⊘
Streamline Float	**Unstreamlined Float**

your core, so that your spine becomes straight. Pull your belly button back toward your spine. Float until you stop. Notice that the distance you travelled is farther still. By creating a firm straight line with your body, you bump into the least water possible, and move through the water in the most streamlined manner. This is the glide or "home base" position for breaststroke.

DRILL FEEDBACK CHART

Problem	Modification
With my face forward, I cannot push off underwater.	Yes, this is an additional drawback of swimming face forward. It is always best to push off the wall completely submerged, to avoid the drag from the waves on the surface of the water.
It is hard to get a strong push off with my feet apart.	Once again, this is an additional drawback of widely positioned feet. For stability on the wall, your feet should be about shoulder width apart. Then when you leave the wall, move your legs together as quickly and smoothly as possible, to bump into the least water possible.
With a straight spine, I am slightly piked at the hips.	Use your straight spine together with your abdominal muscles to create a streamlined body position from head to toe. Sometimes squeezing your buttocks together helps.

52 Rocking Drill

THE PURPOSE OF THIS DRILL
- Using a rocking motion for breaststroke
- Developing unified core action
- Understanding the purpose of rocking

HOW TO DO THIS DRILL

Step 1: Float face down in the water, arms at your sides. Engage your core and straighten your spine. Achieve a "downhill" floating position by pressing your chest down into the water about three inches. Notice that your legs float higher. This resembles the body position during the glide phase of the breaststroke. This is one extreme of the rocking action of the stroke. Hold for five seconds.

Step 2: Now, release your chest press as you draw your heels back toward your buttocks, bending at the knee. Keep your feet under the water. Feel your floating position change. Notice that without raising your chin, your head rises. Your knees should be the lowest point of your float. This resembles the body position when you are approaching the inhale and the power phase of the kick. It is the other extreme of the breaststroke rocking motion. Hold for five seconds.

Step 3: Next, try it with forward momentum. Push off the wall with good force, face down, arms at your sides, core engaged, spine straight. Achieve the glide position immediately by pressing your chest down about three inches. While you are still moving forward, switch to breathing position by releasing your chest and drawing your heels back. Notice that your forward motion slows right away.

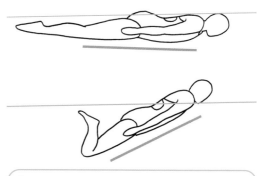

Figure 52 Breaststroke Rocking Motion

Step 4: Again, push off the wall and press your chest down about three inches. Then switch to the breathing position, but this time, quickly shift again, so you are pressing your chest down in the water, your legs are straight, and you regain your glide position. Notice how you can overcome the slowing effect of the breathing position by returning to the advantageous glide position quickly. Try it again. Alternate floating chest down and chest up continuously for several seconds while still moving forward.

153

Step 5: Now, push off the wall with your face down, arms at your sides, core engaged, and spine straight. Begin the rocking motion of the breaststroke, spending twice as much time in the glide position, as in the breathing position. Practice several times. Notice that by returning to the glide position more quickly, you can continue your forward momentum much longer.

DRILL FEEDBACK CHART

Problem	Modification
I can't get back to the glide position.	It is a matter to using your upper body, including your head as a counter-weight to your legs. Hold your core firm, and actively lean forward in the water. Aim to lower your chest more than three inches at first, until you feel your body float "downhill".
I end up going uphill in the breathing position.	The longer you are in the breathing position, the more uphill you will float. Although this position is a necessary part of the breaststroke, for breathing as well as better kicking, it is also a position of drag. It is important to get back to the glide position quickly. Spend half as much time in the breathing position as the glide position.
I am not able to get a breath.	Although your head will rise when you release your chest and draw your heels back, it will probably not rise enough to get a breath until the arm stroke is added later. Concentrate on feeling the change in your body position. When you need a breath, stand and breathe, then resume your floating position.

KICK DRILLS

Unlike other strokes, the kick in the breaststroke produces more forward motion than the arm stroke. It also has a great deal of potential drag. It is a unique kick that uses rounded, lateral and completely splashless leg motion, where the soles of the feet push the water rather than the tops of the feet as in other strokes. The goal of the following breaststroke kicking drills is to experience positioning and, using the hips, knees and feet most advantageously, maximize forward motion, and minimize drag for the most effective breaststroke kick.

Duck Feet

53

THE PURPOSE OF THIS DRILL
* Learning to use your feet as paddles
* Using ankle rotation to keep hold of the water
* Avoiding potential drag

HOW TO DO THIS DRILL

Step 1: Observe a duck swimming in the water. Focus on its feet. They are a perfect swimming feet! They are wide and flexible, and very paddle-like. Looking closely at the kicking motion, although the duck kicks with alternating legs, the actual kicking motion is very similar to the breaststroke kick. Studying the motion of one foot, it shows a good example of how the human foot should move in the breaststroke kick. As the duck's foot prepares for the power phase of the kick, from front to back, it takes a flexed position, forming a right angle to the ankle. During the rounded sweep-back of the duck's kick, notice how the angle of the foot steadily changes, rotating from a flexed and pitched out starting position to a pointed, inwardly pitched position at the end of the kick. This changing foot position, produced by rotating the ankle, allows the duck to maintain pressure on the water most effectively with its foot at all stages of the kick, and create very effective forward motion.

Step 2: Now observe the foot of the duck as it returns to the starting position for another kick. Notice that while the foot is pointed, it appears as it is retracted, reducing the size of the "paddle". It also moves more slowly than during the power phase. This is the recovery of the duck's kick. The duck's foot slides back to the starting position without applying pressure on the water.

Step 3: Keeping the duck's kicking technique in mind, get in the water, at least waist deep, and stand facing the wall of the pool. Hold onto the wall with both hands, arms extended. Draw one foot up behind you, so your heel is close to your buttocks. It should be completely submerged, and remain that way throughout the kick. Flex your foot, creating a right angle at your ankle. Also pitch your toes outward.

Step 4: From this position, press the bottom of your foot against the water. Notice the water resistance on the bottom of your foot when it is flexed. Trace a rounded line with your foot, outward and then inward, until your leg is straight. Try it again with more speed. In order keep your foot pressing against the water as it makes the rounded sweep, the position of your foot must steadily change. Rotate your foot from the ankle to maintain the feeling of water resistance on the bottom of your foot. Practice this several times, increasing speed.

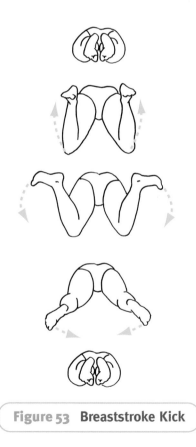

Step 5: When you have achieved steady resistance on the bottom of your foot from the point where your foot starts near your

Figure 53 Breaststroke Kick

156

buttocks, through the rounded sweep, until your leg is straight, then try to mimic the duck's foot recovery. As you bring your foot back up to the starting point, position it so you feel little or no resistance. Slide it through the water smoothly and with less speed. Once it reaches the starting position, flex your foot again and pitch your toes out preparing for another power phase. Practice this several times. Then practice the whole kick, power phase and recovery.

Step 6: Once you are able to feel a difference in the resistance between the power phase and the recovery, try doing the kick with both legs simultaneously. Holding the wall with one arm extended, place the other hand lower on the wall so you can brace yourself easily in a horizontal position. Keep your feet submerged throughout the kick. Your feet should move as mirror images to each other. Draw both heels back toward your buttocks. Focus on using your feet like paddles to engage the water throughout the power phase. Done correctly, by the end of the kick, you should have to tense your arms to prevent yourself from advancing toward the wall. Slide your feet gently back to the starting point, so you don't feel any pull away from the wall. Practice the breaststroke kick several times.

DRILL FEEDBACK CHART

Problem	Modification
My foot makes a splash.	Flex your foot, curling your toes up from the very beginning of the power phase. Kick with the sole of your foot, not the top of your foot as in all other kicks.
I feel resistance on the recovery.	It is important to learn to eliminate as much resistance as you can, because the kick recovery can actually move you backwards done incorrectly. Try keeping your knees still while you move your heels back and up slowly behind you.
I end up with the soles of my feet together by the end of the kick.	You are lucky to have excellent ankle flexibility. When you keep the soles of your feet positioned so they push against the water throughout the rounded sweep, outward, then inward, some people are able to clap the soles of their feet together at the last moment. Make complete use of your flexibility.

Breaststroke Kick on Your Back

THE PURPOSE OF THIS DRILL
- Developing a propulsive kick
- Avoiding folding at the hips
- Positioning your knees inside your feet

HOW TO DO THIS DRILL
Step 1: Lay on your back in the water, hands at your sides, and slightly behind you, fingertips extended. Begin to kick breaststroke kick on your back. Bring your heels back to the point that they touch

your fingertips. Then with your feet flexed and pointed outward, use a quick motion to trace a rounded sweep with your feet, outward then inward, maintaining water pressure on the soles of your feet until your legs are straight. Repeat several times, drawing your heels back slowly and smoothly, then engaging the water with the soles of your feet and pressing firmly against the water until your legs are straight.

Step 2: Now, continuing the same kicking action on your back, focus on your knees. They should remain under the surface of the water as your heels come back and touch your fingertips. If your knees are coming out of the water, it means you are folding at the hips. For many people, this causes a wave of water to wash over their face. If you were swimming on your front doing a breaststroke kick folded at the hips, that wave would work as drag, greatly slowing your forward motion. Try again, maintaining a straight line from your shoulders to your knees. Produce a knee bend by drawing your heels back, rather than by folding at the hips.

Step 3: Still focusing on your knees, positioned under the surface of the water in a straight line from shoulder to knee, position them about shoulder width apart. As you draw your heels back to touch your fingertips, hold the position of your knees steady. Notice that with your knees held still, your feet will be farther apart than your knees when your fingertips touch your heels.

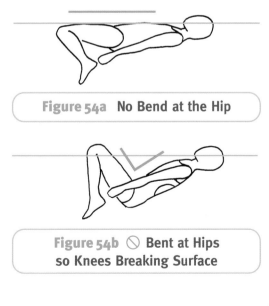

Figure 54a **No Bend at the Hip**

Step 4: Continue your kick, holding your knees steady at shoulder width apart. Trace a rounded sweep with your feet, outward then inward, without your knees

Figure 54b ⊘ **Bent at Hips so Knees Breaking Surface**

moving wider apart. Only at the very end of the kick, as your legs straighten do your knees also move, coming together as the feet also come together. Notice that with firm knees, your lower leg, ankle and foot are rotating around your knees as they sweep out and straighten. Practice again.

Step 5: Once you are able to achieve a kick without folding at the hip, and you are able to maintain a stable knee position, try kicking with more force. You should be able to produce enough forward motion with each kick that you can glide in the straight leg position for three to five seconds before slowing down. Practice this several times.

DRILL FEEDBACK CHART

Problem	Modification
My heels don't touch my fingertips.	Try swinging your heels outward more, when you are drawing your heels back. Remember the heels should be farther apart than the knees.
I get more power when I fold at the hips.	You might, but you also produce much more drag. In fact, kicking this way produces almost as much drag as it does forward motion, so your gain from each kick is practically nothing, as you go forward, then backward. Try using ankle rotation to position your feet, rather than folding at the hip.
My knees are farther apart than my feet.	This could mean you are drawing your feet up the middle. When you do this, you then have to do an additional step of swinging them laterally outward to prepare for the power phase. The drag of wide knees, moving in the opposite direction that you are headed, in addition to the drag of the extra movement to position your feet wide, is hard to overcome. Some swimmers successfully position their knees a bit wider than shoulder width apart, but they still keep them stable through the sweep of the power phase, until the very end when the legs straighten. In addition, their feet remain outside of their knees.

55 Vertical Breaststroke Kick

THE PURPOSE OF THIS DRILL
- Developing a productive kick
- Using foot speed during the power phase
- Eliminating drag

HOW TO DO THIS DRILL

Step 1: In water, at least as deep as you are tall, get into a vertical position. Begin a gentle sculling action (tracing side to side underwater figure eights with your hands) to keep your head above water.

Step 2: To begin the power phase of the breaststroke kick, draw your heels back toward your buttocks. Use flexed feet, stable knees, and kick in a path that your feet rotate around your knees, without producing forward or backwards motion. Use a forceful and quick enough kick so that you bob upward with each kick as your legs straighten. Practice several times, with increasing foot speed.

Step 3: Practice several times. While preparing for the power phase of the kick, avoid raising your knees toward your abdomen so that you don't pull yourself down underwater. Make sure your feet are in the flexed position before beginning the power phase of the kick.

Step 4: Once you have achieved a productive vertical kick, stop the sculling action with your hands. Position your hands: left hand on right shoulder and right hand on left shoulder. Kick, keeping your head above water. Maintain for 30 seconds.

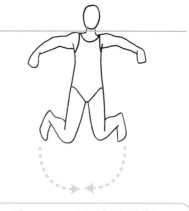

Figure 55 Vertical Kicking

Step 5: When you are able to keep your head up without the help of arm movements, try the advanced version of this drill:

Position your arms so they extend side to side on the surface of the water. Now raise your hands out of the water, bending at a right angle at the elbow. Kick! Can you keep your head up for 30 seconds?

DRILL FEEDBACK CHART

Problem	Modification
I am not bobbing upward.	Use a faster, more forceful sweep, outward then inward with your feet. Make sure you are pushing water with the soles and not the tops of your feet. Also make sure your knees remain stable.
I am sinking.	Practice flexing your feet more, achieving a right angle to your ankle, curling your toes upward, and pitching your feet outward before you kick. You must use the soles of your feet like paddles and achieve constant pressure against the water throughout the power phase in order to stay up. Also, make sure that you are not drawing your knees up toward your abdomen, but drawing your heels up toward your buttocks instead.
This hurts my knees.	Breaststroke kick is not the easiest action for the knees. Modify your knee position so it is comfortable for you. Try adjusting your knees to be slightly farther apart. If it still hurts you, just don't do it.

56 Heads Up Breaststroke Kick

THE PURPOSE OF THIS DRILL
- Using your senses to recognize a productive kick
- Observing momentum
- Practicing an effective kick

HOW TO DO THIS DRILL
Step 1: Push off the wall in a streamlined position, arms extended, clasping one hand over the other. Establish a stable hip position. With your head up, allow your chin to rest on the surface of the water. Begin kicking breaststroke kick, keeping your feet completely submerged throughout each kick.

Step 2: Notice your movement. During the power phase of the kick, you should be able to see your kick producing forward momentum. During the recovery phase of the kick, you should notice no slowing, or movement in the reverse direction. Feel your feet working like paddles during the power phase, pressing on the water. Feel your feet during the recovery, gently slipping back to the starting point without pressing on the water. Listen to your kick. It should not make a sound during the power phase or recovery.

Figure 56a Heads Up Breaststroke Kick

Step 3: Continue kicking with your head up, chin on the water, arms extended to the far end of the pool, looking, listening and feeling. Practice for several lengths of the pool, resting at each end.

Figure 56b Advanced Heads Up Breaststroke Kick

Step 4: Once you are able to produce an effective heads up kick with your arms extended, try the advanced version of this drill. Kick another length, but this time put your arms at your sides, keeping your head up and chin on the surface of the water.

Step 5: Notice that with your arms at your sides, you must use a faster kick, and one with greater force to keep your face above water. Use a forceful kick that gains speed throughout its path, and a gentle recovery, until you can also produce forward momentum for a glide with every kick without your face submerging. Practice for several lengths of the pool, resting at each end.

DRILL FEEDBACK CHART

Problem	Modification
I hear an occasional splash from my feet.	That splash indicates that your feet are not always connected to the water. Check that when you begin your power phase, your feet are flexed, not pointed. Make sure that your spine is not swayed, positioning your hips too high in the water to begin the kick with your feet submerged.
I can't produce a glide.	Make sure you are tracing a rounded path with your feet, outward then inward, not straight back. The breaststroke kick is a large sweeping kick. Make use of the whole thing to produce the most forward momentum.
With my arms down, I can't keep my face up.	This is not easy. As well as using good force during the power phase, your kick must also gain speed all the way until your legs are straight. You must produce little drag during the recovery. Your ankles must be active, adjusting the pitch of the feet throughout the kick. Your knees must be stable, so your lower legs and feet can rotate around them.

ARM STROKE DRILLS

In an effort to overcome drag, and increase forward motion, the breaststroke arm stroke has evolved immensely over time. While it has remained a simultaneous stroke, many theories about what the arms do have been developed. The arm stroke has been described as a heart-shaped pull, a box-shaped pull, even a straight-arm circle, half formed with each arm. It is now accepted that the legs are where the majority of the potential power is in breaststroke, so the arm stroke has evolved into a compact, lateral action, with its main function being to balance the action of the kick, and to facilitate breathing. The goal of the following arm stroke drills for breaststroke is to learn to enhance the breaststroke balance and breathing using a quick, compact arm stroke.

3D Breaststroke Arms 57

THE PURPOSE OF THIS DRILL
* Getting the most out of the arm stroke
* Using an accelerating stroke
* Maintaining a compact stroke

HOW TO DO THIS DRILL

Step 1: Push off the wall for breaststroke. Sweep outward until your hands are slightly outside your shoulders, forming a "Y". Your arms should be straight at this point in the stroke. This is the widest point in the breaststroke arm stroke. From there, sweep your hands inward until they meet under your chin. This is the narrowest point in the breaststroke arm stroke. Practice to the far end of the pool, identifying the wide and the narrow points of the stroke.

Step 2: Again push off the wall for the breaststroke, arms extended. Sweep outward, with your fingertips just below the surface of the

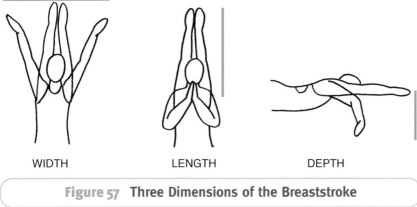

WIDTH　　　　　LENGTH　　　　　DEPTH

Figure 57 **Three Dimensions of the Breaststroke**

water. This is the shallowest point in the breaststroke arm stroke. From there, holding your elbows firm, sweep your hands down and inward, tracing a half circle until your hands meet in the middle, under your chin. This is the deepest point in the breaststroke arm stroke. Practice to the far end of the pool, identifying the shallow and the deep points of the stroke.

Step 3: Again push off the wall for the breaststroke. Start the stroke with your arms completely extended. This is the longest point in the breaststroke arm stroke. Sweep outward, then inward. Your hands meet under your chin. This is the shortest point in the breaststroke arm stroke. Practice to the far end of the pool, identifying the long and the short points of the stroke.

Step 4: Continue swimming breaststroke for several lengths of the pool, observing the three dimensional path of the stroke. Notice the complete area of the arm stroke, by feeling the widest and narrowest points, the shallowest and deepest points, and, the longest and shortest points.

DRILL FEEDBACK CHART

Problem	Modification
I am not producing much forward motion.	Since the breaststroke arm stroke is much more compact than the other strokes, it produces much less forward motion. It is therefore even more important to make the most of the space that you have to work with by applying pressure throughout the three dimensional space.
My elbows don't stay high when I sweep inward.	To make the most of the insweep, it is important to maintain high, still elbows. When your hands meet in the middle, your elbows can fold in toward your sides.
I am not feeling the "Y".	It is important to sweep outward with straight arms, because the insweep that follows uses the longest to shortest dimension of the stroke to accelerate the arm stroke. If your hands have already left the long position during the outsweep, the insweep will be slower and less effective.

Breaststroke Sculling

58

THE PURPOSE OF THIS DRILL
* Learning to use lateral strokes
* Holding on to the water
* Experiencing a high elbow scull

HOW TO DO THIS DRILL
Step 1: Push off the wall, arms extended, face in the water. Use core stability to maintain a good floating position. If necessary, use a gentle but continuous flutter kick. Keeping your hands completely submerged at least two inches under the surface of the water, begin

a sculling action with your hands, maintaining firm wrists. Your hands should be tracing a mirror image of each other. Press the water outward with the palms of your hands, positioning your thumbs lower than your pinkies.

Step 2: After pressing outward just wider than your shoulders, reverse your hand pitch so your thumbs are higher than your pinkies and press the water inward with the palms of your hands.

Step 3: Before your hands meet, again switch the pitch of your hands to thumbs-down and press outward. Produce a continuous lateral sculling action for one minute. To breathe, press your chin forward gently.

Step 4: Increase your hand speed, maintaining high elbows and firm wrists. Trace sideways figure eights with each hand. Practice until you feel you are holding onto the water in both directions, even as you change directions.

Figure 58   Sculling Motion

Step 5: Without increasing the width, depth or length of your scull, and without adding or increasing kicking, attempt to create forward motion with your skull. Use your whole arm to trace your figure eights, maintaining firm wrists, and high elbows. Practice until you can move to the far end of the pool.

DRILL FEEDBACK CHART

Problem	Modification
I am feeling bubbles during my inward scull.	This probably means that your hands are not quite deep enough in the water, and are catching air as you press outward or while changing directions. Keep your hands totally submerged the whole time.
I lose my hold on the water as I change directions.	Think of a knife spreading peanut butter on a slice of bread. Use your hands in the same way, from one side of the bread to the other, and then back again. Also, maintain your hand speed as you change directions.
I am not moving.	Make sure your elbows and wrists are firm. Increase the quickness of your figure eights. Check that your hands are completely submerged.

59 Half-stroke Breaststroke

THE PURPOSE OF THIS DRILL
- Learning to use compact strokes
- Using a quick stroke
- Eliminating drag

HOW TO DO THIS DRILL

Step 1: Push off the wall, preparing to do the breaststroke, arms extended, face in the water. Do four arm strokes with your face in the water, watching your hands as they sweep outward, then inward through the path of the stroke. Return your arms to the fully extended position between each stroke. Kick each time your arms approach straight.

Step 2: Take a breath, then do four more strokes. Reduce the width of your arm stroke until your hands stay within your field of vision throughout the stroke. Still return your arms to the fully extended position between each stroke. Notice that a stroke with less width takes much less time to get your arms back to the extended start position.

Step 3: After breathing, do four more strokes maintaining your reduced arm stroke width. Now, watch your hands as they sweep from shallow to deep through the path of the stroke. Again, return your arms to the fully extended position between each stroke. Kick as your arms approach straight.

Step 4: Take a breath, then do four more strokes, reducing the depth of your stroke so that your hands remain within your field of vision throughout the stroke. Still return your arms to the fully

Figure 59
Half-stroke Breaststroke

extended position between each stroke. Notice that a stroke with less depth takes much less time and effort to get your arms back to the extended start position.

Step 5: Practice the reduced stroke again. Make it compact and quick. It should feel like half a stroke. With your face in the water, your hands should remain easily within your sight throughout the arm stroke.

DRILL FEEDBACK CHART

Problem	Modification
I am not getting any pull from half a stroke.	The point of the drill is to keep your stroke compact, entirely within your field of vision, thereby reducing drag and effort. It is your kick that should produce most of the forward motion.
I can't see my stroke when my hands are under my chest.	Reduce your stroke until you can see your hands the whole time. Keep your hands and elbows in front of your chest.
The arm stroke is now too fast to fit the kick in after each one.	Remember to return to the extended position after each arm stroke. Each arm stroke starts and finishes in that position, giving you more time to kick.

Corners Drill

THE PURPOSE OF THIS DRILL
- Accelerating into the insweep
- Producing lift without pushing down
- Holding onto the water

HOW TO DO THIS DRILL

Step 1: Push off the wall for the breaststroke, arms extended. Press your chest into the water, and use core tension and a straight spine to achieve a "downhill" float. Begin the breaststroke arm stroke, pressing outward with your thumbs low, then inward with your thumbs high. Keep your hands within your range of vision.

Step 2: Do four or five quick strokes, holding on to the water throughout the entire path of the stroke, especially during the transition from outsweep to insweep. It is very important to maintain firm wrists and high elbows during this transition. It should feel like you are turning tight corners with each arm. It is important to feel that you are doing so with your whole arms, not just your hands. Upon arriving at these corners, gather speed for the insweep. Increase your speed as you round the corners. At the end of each insweep, when your hands come together in the middle, push them straight ahead to the extended position.

Step 3: Notice that with a quick enough arm stroke, which accelerates at the corners, you feel the effects of lift, without ever pushing down on the water. Try it again. Increase the speed of your stroke so that you produce noticeable lift in your upper body as your hands transition from outsweep to insweep. Without altering your head position, your face will rise

Figure 60 The Corners

174

as you begin your quick insweep. Notice that if you maintain a firm core, when your upper body rises, your feet will drop just a bit. Use this opportunity, when your face is naturally at its highest out of the water to get a breath. Then return your face to the water as your hands approach the extended position. Press your chest downward.

Step 4: Continue practicing your quick lateral arm stroke, accelerating at the corners to produce lift. Then, quickly return to the "downhill" position. Spend half as much time in the breathing position as in the glide position.

DRILL FEEDBACK CHART

Problem	Modification
I don't produce any lift.	Try increasing the speed of your hand at the corners. Maintain your core tension and straight spine, so that when your upper body rises, your feet drop a bit. If your core is not unified, your hips will actually limit the lift effects your arms can achieve at the corners.
I don't feel the corners.	If the transition from outsweep to insweep is too gradual, you will not feel it or benefit from it. Make it a tight corner, and accelerate your hands through it. Also make sure you are changing the pitch of your hands, going into the corners with your thumbs down, and coming out with your thumbs up.
I can't get back to the glide position.	As your arms begin to extend, and your face returns to the water, drop your chest lower into the water. Make sure you are looking at the bottom of the pool and not forward.

61 Hand Speed Drill

THE PURPOSE OF THIS DRILL
- Observing a compact arm stroke
- Using a quick arm stroke
- Holding on to the water

HOW TO DO THIS DRILL
Step 1: Push off the wall, arms extended, face forward out of the water, chin on the surface. Use core tension to maintain a good

floating position. Begin doing the breaststroke arm stroke, accompanied by a very quick flutter kick. Look down at your hands just below the surface of the water as you do the breaststroke arm stroke. Keep the entire stroke within your range of vision.

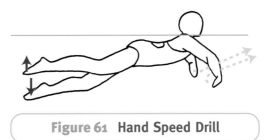

Figure 61 Hand Speed Drill

Step 2: Check for firm wrists and high elbows, especially at the corners. Practice until you feel you are holding on to the water in both directions. Start each new stroke from an extended arm position.

Step 3: Still focusing on your hands, increase the rate of your arm stroke. Pick up speed through the corners and into the insweep. Practice until your arms are accelerating through the entire stroke. Your stroke should be moving fast enough so that you can clap your hands under your chin at the end of the insweep. Then, quickly return your arms to the starting point, fully extended.

Step 4: Now focus on your quick flutter kick. Kick at a rate of at least one down-beat per second. Try to accomplish an entire arm stroke during three to four kicks. Watch your hands, checking that you are maintaining a compact stroke, firm wrists and high elbows, and accelerating into the insweep. When your hands return to the extended position, hold them there for six kicks before trying to do another complete arm stroke within the time of three to four kicks.

Step 5: Continue practicing to the far end of the pool. Focus on the speed of your hands throughout each arm stroke, then return to the extended position and hold. Start each arm stroke from this still position, then attempt to go from zero to sixty within the time of three or four kicks.

DRILL FEEDBACK CHART

Problem	Modification
Water wells up in the middle at the end of my insweep.	This shows that you have a good hold on the water, and are using good hand speed. Just make sure that you are not lifting that water upward, or you will be creating drag. When your hands meet at the end of your insweep, that is the end of the power phase, so just let go of the water and return your hands to the extended position.
It's hard to keep my head up.	Use core tension to lean "downhill" from hips to chest. Make sure you are not trying to keep your head too high out of the water. This stroke produces very few waves, so your mouth just barely has to clear the water. Also make sure you are pitching your hands thumbs-down for the outsweep, and thumbs-up for the insweep, and using a quick and accelerating stroke.
This is awkward with the flutter kick.	The flutter kick is meant to work like a metronome to help you achieve a quicker arm stroke. It also should allow you to fully focus more on the productivity of the arm stroke alone, without any assistance from the breaststroke kick.

Breaststroke with Fists

62

THE PURPOSE OF THIS DRILL
- Learning to feel the water with the forearm
- Understanding the changing elbow position
- Appreciating the role of the hand

HOW TO DO THIS DRILL

Step 1: Push off the wall as if preparing to do the regular breaststroke. Before the first stroke, form closed fists with each hand.

Step 2: Start the arm stroke. At first it may seem impossible to make forward progress without the paddles of your open hands. Stroke quickly, purposely positioning your arms so that the inside of your forearms press against the water throughout the arm stroke. This will require you to initiate your stroke with your arms extended, but elbows rotated high, then to maintain firm elbows while your fists sweep outward.

Step 3: Accelerate the stroke maintaining high elbows as you turn the corners with your fists. Keep the stroke speed quick. Adapt your stroke to the handless paddle. When your hands approach the end of the insweep, then allow your elbows to fold inward in front of your rib cage, still pressing against the water with your forearms. Practice the change of elbow position again, letting your elbows come inward, but not back like chicken wings, and only at the end of the insweep. Continue to the far end of the pool.

Figure 62
Breaststroke With Fists

179

Step 4: Now push off again, this time with open hands. Swim regular breaststroke, using your hands as well as your forearms to press against the water in both directions. Do a quick, accelerating stroke. Keep high elbows until the last part of the insweep.

Step 5: Continue alternating lengths of fists and open hands until you are feeling the water with a paddle that includes both your hand and your forearm.

DRILL FEEDBACK CHART

Problem	Modification
I am not moving.	Reposition your forearm so when your arm moves through the stroke, the inside of your forearm presses constantly against the water in both directions.
I am getting a lot of bubbles in my outsweep.	Make sure that your wrists are not pitched backwards. There should be a straight line from your elbow to your knuckles. Also, make sure that your entire fist is submerged so you don't pull air down into the water.
My elbows end up back like chicken wings.	This indicates your arms are stroking in the collapsed position. Work on keeping your elbows high through the entire outsweep corners and then draw your elbows firmly together just in front of your rib cage.

RECOVERY DRILLS

Breaststroke is the only stroke with a recovery that passes through the water rather than over it, leading to the potential for a great deal of drag. To overcome this drag, the breaststroke recovery must be an active part of the stroke, rather than a resting phase, as in other strokes. The resting phase in the breaststroke comes after the recovery, during the glide. Some swimmers have tried to avoid drag by developing over-the-water recovery styles, with varying degrees of success. For the most part, swimmers have chosen to overcome the drag of the traditional in water recovery by increasing speed into, and streamlining during and after the recovery. The goal of the following breaststroke recovery drills is to minimize drag by quickening the transition between arm stroke and recovery, and developing a long, fast and compact recovery that works with the line of the stroke.

Growing Your Recovery

63

THE PURPOSE OF THIS DRILL
- Achieving the longest recovery
- Using your elbows to extend recovery
- Using your chest to extend recovery

HOW TO DO THIS DRILL
Step 1: Stand in waist deep water, facing the pool wall. Bow forward so that your chin is on the surface the water. Look down and forward, preparing to watch your breaststroke arm stroke and recovery. Extend your arms in front of you so your fingertips touch the wall. Your hands should be slightly submerged in the water. Now, begin the arm stroke, compact, quick through the corners, maintaining firm wrists throughout, and high elbows until the last part of the insweep. When your hands finish the insweep, return them to the extended position, fingertips touching the wall in front of you.

181

Step 2: Take one step back – the length of your foot. Maintaining your chin on the surface of the water, do another breaststroke arm stroke, compact, quick through the corners, firm wrists throughout, high elbows until the last part of the insweep. At the end of the insweep, form a point with the fingertips of both hands, and drive your hands and elbows forward with speed. As your hands reach toward the wall, bring your forearms as close together as possible. Your arms should form a long arrowhead, from hands to shoulders. Notice that simply by straightening your arms more and creating a narrow leading edge with your hands, forearms and elbows, you have increased the length of your recovery, and are able to touch the wall.

Step 3: Take another step back – the length of your foot. With your chin still on the surface of the water, do another breaststroke arm stroke, compact, quick at the corners, firm wrists, high elbows. At the end of the insweep, with your fingertips together and pointed forward, drive your hands and elbows forward with speed, narrowing the space between your forearms as you reach. Before your hands have reached full extension, drop your chest down and forward into the water as you reach for the wall. Notice that using your chest in the recovery action, you have increased the length of your recovery even more, and are able to touch the wall.

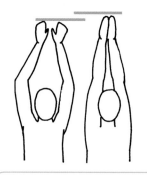

Figure 63a
Grow Your Recovery by
Straightening Elbows

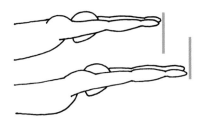

Figure 63a
Grow Your Recovery by
Dropping Your Chest

Step 4: Now practice growing your recovery while swimming. Push off the wall face down, achieving a firm core and good floating position. Begin the breaststroke arm stroke. As your hands finish the insweep, return your arms to the front extended position, making a tight arrow with your arms. Drive your hands and elbows forward, bringing your forearms as close together as you can. With your arms forming a narrow leading edge, drop your chest down into the water. Do a breaststroke kick as your chest drops. Feel your body move forward in a streamlined glide. Hold that position for three to five seconds before starting another stroke. Continue to the far end of the pool.

DRILL FEEDBACK CHART

Problem	Modification
I can't get my elbows very close together.	Everyone's flexibility is different. Just get your elbows closer than they were originally. You can also try placing your hands palms together during recovery and see if this moves your forearms closer.
When I use my chest, I lose my footing and fall forward.	This actually shows that you have succeeded in shifting your weight forward for encouraging a more productive glide, as well as a longer recovery. Keep it up!
When I drop my chest into the water, my face submerges.	You might be dropping your chest too far downward. Try it again with less depth. Try to make your chest join the forward motion of your arms as they extend forward.

64 Shoot to Streamline

THE PURPOSE OF THIS DRILL
- Learning to accelerate into the recovery
- Recovering with the rocking motion of the stroke
- Eliminating any pause between insweep and recovery

HOW TO DO THIS DRILL

Step 1: Push off the wall, preparing to do the breaststroke, your arms extended fully in front of you, forming the point of an arrow from your hands to your shoulders. Achieve a "downhill" floating position. Begin a compact arm stroke, that is quick through the corners.

Step 2: Maintain firm wrists throughout the stroke, and high elbows until the last part of the insweep, when your elbows fold inward in front of your rib cage. As your elbows fold in, notice that your hands come together in a sort of praying position. This is the breaststroke breathing position, a necessary but drag-producing point in the stroke.

Step 3: Getting back to the "downhill" position quickly is crucial in retaining your hard-earned forward momentum. To achieve this, the recovery must continue the forward motion of the breaststroke, avoiding any pause after the insweep. From the "praying position", shoot your hands and elbows forward at lightning speed, with your forearms close together as you drop your chest and head down forward. Kick when your arms are in mid-recovery. Glide for three to five seconds in a fully streamlined position.

Step 4: Do another stroke. Use a quick outsweep, and a quicker insweep. Make the recovery quickest of all. Do it again, accelerating through the entire

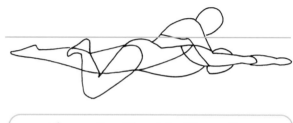

Figure 64 **Shoot to Streamline**

stroke, then shooting your arms forward in the recovery. Notice that the narrower your recovery is, the faster it cuts through the water. Notice too, that by eliminating any pause in the "praying position", the recovering arms add to the forward momentum of the arm stroke.

Step 5: Continue practicing the narrowest recovery possible, eliminating any stall between the insweep and the recovery. Keep practicing until your arm stroke and recovery have become one continuous, accelerating action. Catch the forward momentum of the stroke and shoot to the streamline. Glide for three to five seconds after each recovery.

DRILL FEEDBACK CHART

Problem	Modification
I have a pause in the "praying position".	To avoid the slowing effects of drag, it is very important not to pause in this position. Make sure that you are preparing to breathe at the corners and not later, or you can get stuck in an "uphill" position, and miss the opportunity to time your recovery to the forward motion of the stroke.
My hands end up palms together at the end of the recovery.	That is fine. It is also fine if your palms face down. Either way, after gliding, you will turn your palms outward to begin the arm stroke. The bottom line is that for a streamlined recovery, the arms and hands should slice through the water and form a narrow leading edge in front of your body.
My recovery aims "uphill".	Be sure your arms are aligned forward from the shoulders, elbows and wrists. Check the direction your fingertips are pointing at the end of your recovery. It should be forward, not upward.

Fold and Shrug

THE PURPOSE OF THIS DRILL
- Adding speed to the recovery
- Increasing momentum into the glide
- Learning to rest after the recovery

HOW TO DO THIS DRILL

Step 1: Push off the wall preparing to swim breaststroke, arms extended. Achieve the "downhill" floating position. Begin your arm stroke, sweeping out, then accelerate around the corners, and in towards the middle to the "praying position" before recovery. This is also the point in the stroke when you draw your heels up toward your buttocks, preparing to start the power phase of your kick. In this position, your head and chest should be higher than your hips. You have a brief window of opportunity for breathing between the corners and the praying position.

Step 2: As your elbows fold quickly inward to the "praying position", shrug your shoulders up. Then, as you transition to your quick, narrow recovery, shrug your shoulders forward and down. Notice that with this shoulder shrug, your upper body becomes more involved in the recovery. Kick as your arms approach the streamlined position. Glide and rest for three to five seconds.

Step 3: Do another stroke. Accelerate through the outsweep corners and insweep. Fold your elbow in at the end of the insweep and shrug your shoulders up, then forward and down into the recovery. Notice that the shrug helps keep your momentum going through the "praying position", where a disadvantageous pause often occurs. As you shoot your hands and forearms forward, and drop your chest down and forward, notice too that your recovery carries more speed. Kick as your arms approach the streamlined position. Glide and rest for three to five seconds.

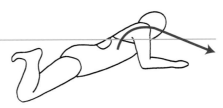

Figure 65a Fold and Shrug

Step 4: Do another stroke. Quick outsweep, turn the corners and accelerate into the insweep. Approach the "praying position and shrug your shoulders up as your elbows fold in front of your chest, then down and forward giving more speed to the recovery. Notice that you are able to achieve a greater

Figure 65b Without Fold and Shrug

"downhill" streamline with the shrug helping to shift your weight forward. Glide and rest for three to five seconds.

Step 5: Continue to practice for several lengths of the pool. Sweep out, then in. Fold and shrug. Feel the momentum of the stroke follow your arms into their recovery and glide.

DRILL FEEDBACK CHART

Problem	Modification
The shrug helps me go up, but not forward.	You have to shrug your shoulders up and then forward and down to feel it assist in the speed of the recovery. Try it on land first, in the mirror. With your arms at your sides, shrug your shoulders up, then roll them forward and down. Now trace the path of your stroke in the air, adding the shrug up then forward and down, as you go through the "praying position". Feel the shrug forward add momentum to your recovery and glide.
My elbows fold into my rib cage, not in front of it.	Try beginning the shrug earlier, before your elbows fold in too far. Also make sure that your elbows are high and firm coming into the insweep, and remain high until the last few seconds.
My streamline is flat, not "downhill".	Make sure you are looking at the bottom of the pool and not forward during your streamline. Also, realize that the degree of the "downhill" float is very subtle. It shouldn't be so severe that you are aiming at the bottom of the pool, or so deep that you have to lift yourself up to the surface with the next stroke. As long as your chest is slightly lower than your hips, you have achieved a "downhill" position, and will move forward better during the glide than if your hips and chest were equal in depth, or worse, that your hips were the lowest part of your float.

BREATHING DRILLS

The forward breathing style of the breaststroke makes the head position a factor in maintaining the forward line of the stroke. In addition, the timing of the breathing is crucial in reducing drag during the power phase of the stroke. Incorrectly timed, the breathing can break the forward motion of the stroke, but timed well, the breathing action can actually improve it. The goal of the following breathing drills is to learn the correct timing of the breaststroke breathing and to unify the head and body into a single action that benefits the stroke.

Inhale at the High Point

THE PURPOSE OF THIS DRILL
- Learning the correct timing of the inhale
- Breathing with the line of the stroke
- Feeling lift

HOW TO DO THIS DRILL
Step 1: Push off the wall preparing to swim breaststroke, arms extended. Achieve the "downhill" floating position. Begin your arm stroke, sweeping out, maintaining firm wrists and high elbows. Hold on to the water as you accelerate into the corners, maintaining a firm spine all the way through your neck. As your hands round the corners, preparing to sweep inward quickly, feel your body position change, and your upper body rise. Notice that without raising your chin, your mouth clears the water. Use this opportunity to inhale. As you recover and kick, notice that you regain the "downhill" position, and your face returns to the water.

Step 2: Do another stroke. Sweep your hands outward and into the corners. As your hands change directions at the corners, feel the lift produced for your head and upper body. Your breathing window occurs when your mouth clears the water, through the high point in the stroke, near the praying position. When you transition into the recovery, and back to the "downhill" position, allow your face to drop into the water with the rest of your upper body as you kick.

Step 3: Continue stroking. Allow your face to rise with each stroke cycle, as your stroke produces lift. Inhale at the high point in the stroke until your face returns to the water as you kick, with the forward line of the recovery.

Step 4: Continue practicing until you achieve your inhale as your face naturally rises to its high point. Then, allow your face to return to the water without creating any pause in the stroke.

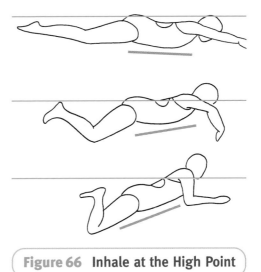

Figure 66 Inhale at the High Point

191

DRILL FEEDBACK CHART

Problem	Modification
I don't produce enough lift to get a breath.	Make sure that when approaching the corners you are accelerating through. Also, it is important at this point to draw your heels back, to achieve lift for your upper body.
I am inhaling before the corners.	Although you can catch a breath at this point in the stroke by raising your chin, doing so compromises the forward line of the stroke as your head tilts back, in effect, putting on the brakes.
My inhale is in the praying position.	Try accelerating out of the corners more to increase your natural lift. Beginning your inhale in the praying position encourages a drag-producing pause before the recovery.

Eyes on the Water

THE PURPOSE OF THIS DRILL
- Maintaining a stable head position
- Breathing with the line of the stroke
- Avoiding a nodding breathing style

HOW TO DO THIS DRILL
Step 1: Push off the wall preparing to swim breaststroke. Achieve the "downhill" floating position, arms extended. Focus on maintaining a straight spine, from your hips through your neck. You should be looking at the bottom of the pool, not forward. Begin your arm stroke, sweeping out, and holding on to the water as you accelerate into the corners. As your hands move quickly round the corners, and you feel lift, allow your face to rise, focusing your eyes

down at the water right in front of you the whole time. Inhale. Still maintaining your firm spine, return your face to the water as you recover and kick. Exhale.

Step 2: Do another stroke. Inhale at the corners, looking at the water directly in front of you. As you finish your inhale, you should be able to see your hands move into the recovery. You should not be able to see the far end of the pool. As you kick, your face should drop down between your arms, and without changing your chin position, you should again be looking at the bottom of the pool as you exhale.

Step 3: Continue stroking, maintaining a straight spine line through your neck. Avoid any nodding action as you breathe with each stroke. As your face rises to inhale, keep your eyes on the water right in front of you. Watch your hands move into the recovery. Regain your "downhill" position as you kick, letting your face return to the water without

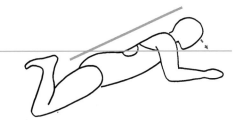

Figure 67a Looking at the Water While Breathing

Figure 67b ⃠ Looking Ahead While Breathing

any independent head movement. Exhale and glide, looking at the bottom of the pool.

Step 4: Practice to the far end of the pool, maintaining a stable head position, looking down at the water during breathing, and at the bottom of the pool during the glide.

DRILL FEEDBACK CHART

Problem	Modification
I can't glide downhill unless I lower my chin during the recovery.	If you chin starts in a low position, you would not have to lower it during the recovery. Use a quick arm stroke to achieve lift to breathe while looking at water. Then, drop your chest down and forward, as you move into the recovery. Your shoulder shrug will also help you transition to the "downhill" position. This way your head and body will work together to maintain the forward line of the stroke.
I can't tell where I am in the pool.	Look at the line on the bottom of the pool. There should be a "T" as you are approaching the wall. Then you will be able to use your peripheral vision to see the wall while maintaining a beneficial stable head position.
My head goes back into the water before my hands recover.	You might be inhaling too early in the stroke. Or your hands could be moving too slowly. However, this shows you are looking at the water! Inhale only when you feel lift at the corners, and sweep quickly inward, then without a pause, shoot into the recovery. As your arms form an arrow beyond your face, there is a perfect space for your head to return to the water between your arms as you kick.

Tennis Ball Drill

68

THE PURPOSE OF THIS DRILL

- Maintaining a stable head position
- Breathing with the lift of the stroke
- Achieving lift by dropping the hips

HOW TO DO THIS DRILL

Step 1: Place a tennis ball under your chin and hold it there, maintaining a straight spine all the way up through your neck. This will require you to adjust the position of the tennis ball out from your throat, holding on to it with the point of your chin. Check in a mirror to insure your spine-line is not compromised.

Step 2: Push off the wall preparing to swim breaststroke, holding the tennis ball with your chin. Achieve the "downhill" floating position, arms extended. In order to avoid dropping the tennis ball, look at the bottom of the pool. Begin your arm stroke, sweeping out, and accelerate into the corners. As your hands quickly round the corners and you achieve lift, inhale without dropping the tennis ball. Return your face to the water as you recover and kick. Exhale.

Step 3: Do another stroke. Accelerate your arm stroke to achieve lift. Maintaining a firm hip position, draw your heels back toward your buttocks, and breathe when your head is naturally at the highest point in the stroke. Hold on to the tennis ball and inhale from the corners through the praying position. As you recover and kick, press your chest down, allowing your face to return to the water without dropping the tennis ball.

Figure 68
Breaststroke with a Tennis Ball

Step 4: Once you have succeeded in doing a stroke without dropping the tennis ball, try three strokes in a row. Maintain stable hips and a straight spine-line through your neck. Use an accelerating arm stroke as you draw your heels back to achieve lift to inhale. Regain your "downhill" position as your recover and kick, looking down at the water and pressing your chest down for the glide.

Step 5: Repeat this drill over several practices, until you are able to hold on to the tennis ball for an entire length of the pool.

DRILL FEEDBACK CHART

Problem	Modification
I don't get enough lift to breathe.	Make sure you are using a productive sculling action, outward then inward, accelerating your hands throughout the stroke.
I drop the ball at the corners.	This probably means you are raising your chin at this point. Instead, look down and accelerate your insweep faster to clear the water for the inhale.
I drop the ball during recovery.	You are probably looking forward, not down during recovery. Use your chest to achieve your glide position, rather than your head. Making this change will improve your glide productivity, because you will have less frontal resistance.

LEVERAGE DRILLS

Improvements in breaststroke across the board, over the past twenty years, are largely due to rule changes that allow better use of leverage and the elimination of drag. By producing an integrated rocking motion between the head and legs, with the hips as stable as possible in the middle, the productivity of the arm stroke, kick and glide is increased, and points of potential drag are minimized. A good rocking motion does not have to be extreme to be effective, it just has to be a unified body action, so each stroke action works as a counterbalance to the others. Using a rocking motion allows the swimmer to inhale when more water covers the feet. Using a rocking motion allows the swimmer to transition to recovery more quickly, avoiding drag. The purpose of the following drills for leverage in the breaststroke is to learn to use a rocking motion to create better leverage and less drag in the stroke.

Breaststroke with Dolphin

69

THE PURPOSE OF THIS DRILL
* Developing a productive rocking motion
* Maintaining a firm core
* Developing a rhythmic stroke

HOW TO DO THIS DRILL
Step 1: Push off the wall preparing to swim breaststroke, arms extended, looking at the bottom of the pool. Maintaining a firm core, do six good full-body dolphin kicks. Avoid over-bending at the knee, and allow each kick to whip down from high in your body down to your feet. As you move through the water, notice how the dolphin action positions your body similar to the rocking motion of the breaststroke.

Step 2: After six kicks, add the breaststroke arm stroke. Sweep out toward the corners as you snap your feet downward. The combined actions of your quick insweep and the downbeat of the dolphin

197

should enable you to feel lift at this point, so you are able to achieve your inhale.

Step 3: Without any pause in your arm stroke, finish your insweep and kick again as you shoot through the recovery. The combined action of a quick, narrow recovery, and the downbeat of the dolphin, should enable you to regain your "downhill" position.

Step 4: Do another stroke. Kick down as your hands approach their widest point, and down again as your hands go into the fast recovery.

Step 5: Do several strokes in a row. Use a rhythmic dolphin, and produce two evenly spaced down-beats to each arm stroke. One kick should give you lift to achieve breathing. The other should add to the speed of your recovery, so you achieve a productive glide.

Step 4: Practice more until you can feel a rhythmic rocking motion that assists the other actions of the stroke.

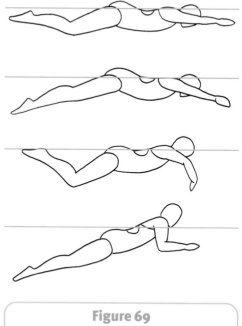

Figure 69
Breaststroke with Dolphin

DRILL FEEDBACK CHART

Problem	Modification
I am not rocking.	Make sure your dolphin action goes through the entire length of your body, not just through your lower legs. Allow your chest to be low through the recovery, and high during breathing.
I lose the rhythm after a few strokes.	It does take practice. Focus on the timing the down-beat of your two kicks to the two key points in the arm stroke: the widest point and the narrowest point. When you lose the rhythm, stand up and start again.
I get stuck in the praying position.	This could mean that your kicks are both happening before that point. One kick should occur as you turn the corners, so you have speed going through the praying position. The next kick helps you regain a downhill float.

Breaststroke Alternating Dolphin and Breaststroke Kick

THE PURPOSE OF THIS DRILL
- Using dolphin action in the breaststroke
- Transferring power through the rocking action of the stroke
- Practicing a productive rocking action

HOW TO DO THIS DRILL
Step 1: Push off the wall, preparing to swim breaststroke. Achieve a straight spine and streamlined position. Begin the breaststroke arm stroke, sweeping out to the corners. Inhale with the insweep. Do one good full-body dolphin at the corners, and another one as you shoot

your hands forward into a narrow, streamlined recovery. Glide.

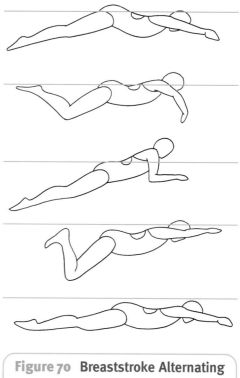

Step 2: Begin the next arm stroke. Sweep your hands out, round the corners and inhale as you do the insweep. This time, do one good breaststroke kick as you shoot your hands forward into a narrow, streamlined recovery. Glide.

Step 3: Continue swimming breaststroke alternating dolphin and breaststroke kick. Accelerate your arm stroke so the insweep merges seamlessly into the recovery. Your hands should arrive in the streamlined position before the kick finishes. Notice that by doing so you

Figure 70 Breaststroke Alternating Dolphin and Breaststroke Kick

achieve a good "downhill" streamline, and productive glide with both kinds of kick. Notice too that the rocking motion of the stroke works the same with both kicks.

Step 4: Keep swimming breaststroke alternating dolphin and breaststroke kick. On the stroke with breaststroke kick, there is one arm stroke and one kick per stroke. On the stroke with dolphin kick, there is one arm stroke to two kicks. Notice, though, that when doing the stroke with the breaststroke kick, a dolphin-like downbeat becomes apparent in the hips, as you transition to recovery.

Step 5: Keep practicing, allowing the rocking motion of the stroke to transfer power through your body, with dolphin as well as with breaststroke kick. Once you are producing good glide momentum with both dolphin and breaststroke kick, alternate laps of the drill and regular breaststroke. Feel the rocking motion transfer power to the rest of the body like with the dolphin.

DRILL FEEDBACK CHART

Problem	Modification
My head bounces with the dolphin kick.	Make sure that you are maintaining a firm spine, so that when you do a dolphin down-beat, your upper body goes up, instead of bouncing.
I can't get the rhythm.	This is not an easy drill, but with practice, you will master it. Start with the breaststroke kick, noticing exactly when you start the power phase of the kick in relation to the recovery. On the next stroke, start your dolphin down-beat at the same point.
I am missing the streamline when using.	Make sure you are not over-bending at the knee. Use stable hips to do the dolphin kick. Generate the power for the dolphin kick, and let it roll down through the entire length of your leg, and up through your chest as your arm reaches for the streamline. Hold your hands together and count to three before starting the next arm stroke.

71 Stroke Up to Breathe, Kick Down to Glide

THE PURPOSE OF THIS DRILL
- Feeling a productive rocking motion
- Maintaining the forward line of the stroke
- Avoiding flat breaststroke

HOW TO DO THIS DRILL

Step 1: Push off the wall preparing to swim breaststroke, arms extended, looking at the bottom of the pool. Maintain a firm spine and achieve a "downhill" floating position by pressing your chest downward. Begin your arm stroke, sweeping out and into the corners. Allow your chest to rise as you round the corners, and as you accelerate the insweep, feel your face clear the water. Use this part of the stroke, from the corners through the insweep to inhale as you move forward.

Step 2: As you transition to the recovery, your heels should be in a position close to your buttocks preparing for the power phase of the kick. When your hands pass your face during the recovery, kick with force, and feel your head and upper body return to the water. Use this power phase of the kick to achieve a productive glide. Hold for three to five seconds.

Step 3: Do another stroke. Feel your body achieve the breathing position during your arm stroke. Feel your body position change back to the "downhill" position as you kick. Notice the absence of a flat floating position.

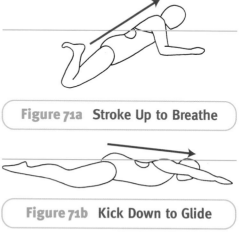

Figure 71a Stroke Up to Breathe

Figure 71b Kick Down to Glide

Step 4: Do several strokes in a row. Stroke up to breathe, kick down to glide, all the time moving forward. Practice until you are able to achieve a quick inhale with your arm stroke, and a productive glide following your kick, spending twice as much time in the "downhill" position as in the breathing position.

DRILL FEEDBACK CHART

Problem	Modification
I don't glide well.	Make sure you are using flexed feet to kick, and that your feet are following a rounded path, outward and then inward. Also make sure you are transitioning to recovery before you kick, so you can start shifting your weight forward and down, then achieve a more productive glide with the power from your kick.
I am floating flat.	Make sure you are maintaining a firm spine and not nodding to breathe. Doing so collapses the leverage effect in the stroke, making you swim flat.
My feet come out of the water.	This could mean you are not maintaining a straight spine during breathing, but rocking your head back as you lift your chin. The consequence of doing this can be a swayed back and high hips, making your feet come out of the water. It could also mean that your feet are not flexed just before the power phase of the kick.

COORDINATION DRILLS

Of all four competitive strokes, breaststroke requires the most precise coordination to overcome the inherent drag in the stroke, in order to produce good forward motion. By correctly sequencing and balancing the actions of the arm stroke, breathing, kick and glide, each individual action of the stroke works better. The following drills for breaststroke coordination focus on the inter-related actions of the stroke, how they overlap, and work together to create an effective stroke.

72 No Stars

THE PURPOSE OF THIS DRILL
- Using the most efficient breaststroke timing
- Avoiding drag
- Using the arm then the legs

HOW TO DO THIS DRILL
Step 1: Push off the wall for the breaststroke, arms extended. Look at the bottom of the pool and achieve a straight spine. Notice how well you move through the water in this narrow, streamlined position.

Step 2: Begin to swim breaststroke to the far end of the pool. Use a quick stroke tempo with both your arms and your legs. After several strokes, freeze at the point in the stroke when your hands are at their widest. Notice where your feet are. They should be at their narrowest point.

Step 3: Continue swimming breaststroke, and resume your quick stroke tempo. After several strokes, freeze at the point when your feet are at their widest. Notice where your hands are. They should be at their narrowest point.

Step 4: If your hands and feet are wide at the same time, this puts you in the star position, the most disadvantageous way to move through the water. The star position is achieved when your arms and legs are in their power phase at the same time. In this position, the arm and the leg action cancel each other out, and you produce little or no forward motion. Swim breaststroke again, checking for the star position.

Step 5: To avoid the star position, your kick must follow your arm stroke with very little overlap. Begin the power phase of the legs only when your arms are well into the recovery. Try it. Push off the wall for the breaststroke. Sweep your hands out toward the corners, actively holding your ankles together in the extended position. As your arms sweep in and you breathe at the high point in the stroke, draw your heels back gently toward your buttocks. Shoot your arms into streamline without any pause. As your arms approach their narrow point forward, then kick.

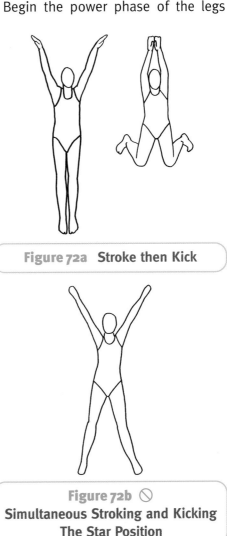

Figure 72a   Stroke then Kick

Figure 72b ⊘
**Simultaneous Stroking and Kicking
The Star Position**

Step 6: Continue swimming breaststroke, performing your arm stroke and then your kick. Keep your legs still during the power phase of your arms, and your arms still during the power phase of your legs. You will achieve the best forward motion in breaststroke if you stagger the wide points of the stroke. Time your stroke so that feet are narrow when your arms are wide, and, your arms are narrow when your feet are wide. Achieve total streamline with your whole body before starting the next stroke.

DRILL FEEDBACK CHART

Problem	Modification
My kick starts as my arm stroke recovery starts.	Try to hold your kick even longer so that you can avoid your recovery action working against your kick action.
I can achieve a more continuous stroke with my arms and legs stroking at the same time.	Breaststroke is unique in that it is not a continuous stroke. By doing arm then leg action, you will produce more forward motion with less effort, and be able to rest during the glide phase.
I never achieve total streamline.	Total streamline will allow you to ride the momentum of your previous stroke. If you start your next stroke before you have achieved total streamline, you will be working harder than you need to.

Stroke, Breathe, Kick, Glide Mantra   73

THE PURPOSE OF THIS DRILL
- Learning the correct sequence of stroke actions
- Avoiding cancelling out the effect of one stroke action with another
- Practicing the correct timing of the breaststroke

HOW TO DO THIS DRILL
Step 1: Visualize the breaststroke in your mind. Say to yourself the steps in sequence of the breaststroke: stroke, breathe, kick, glide. Say it again. Stroke, breathe, kick, gliiiiiiiide, drawing out the word glide, so it takes as much time to say as the three previous steps combined. Match each step in the sequence to the breaststroke in

your mind. "Stroke" refers to the arm stroke, outsweep, corners and insweep. "Breathe" refers to the inhale. "Kick" refers to the power phase of the kick. "Glide" refers to the streamlined float that maximizes the momentum of the stroke.

Step 2: Push off the wall, preparing to swim breaststroke, straight spine, streamlined position. Say the steps in the sequence to yourself again as you glide forward. Now perform the stroke actions in slow motion, repeating the sequence of steps in your mind, beginning each action when you say that step. Correctly timed, the glide should take as long as the other three actions of the stroke combined. Stroke, breathe, kick, gliiiiiiiide.

Step 3: Do another stroke, again matching the start of each action to the step as you say it to yourself. If you are following the stroke sequence correctly, your arm stroke and inhale should be finished before you begin the power phase of your kick. So, you could modify the mantra to be "Stroke, breathe, then kick, gliiiiiide.

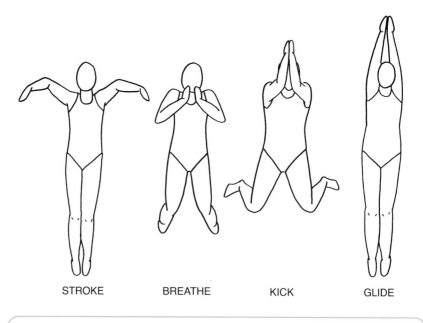

STROKE   BREATHE   KICK   GLIDE

Figure 73 Stroke, Breathe, Kick, Glide Mantra

Step 4: Keep practicing, and repeating to yourself the stroke sequence and timing mantra. Once you are able to perform each stroke action in order, increase your stroke rate. Notice that while the arm stroke starts first, the breathing overlaps with the insweep of the arm stroke. So, you could modify the mantra to be "Stroke and breathe, then kick, gliiiiiide." The "and" marks the corners of the arm stroke.

Step 5: Keep practicing and repeating the mantra. Notice that your arms will have already reached the extended position when your kick finishes, and your body reaches streamline. So, you could modify the mantra to be "Stroke and breathe, then kick and gliiiiiide." The second "and" marks the point when the feet come together at the end of the kick.

Step 6: Continue practicing with the fully developed mantra giving sequence and timing to your stroke. "Stroke and breathe, then kick and gliiiiiide."

DRILL FEEDBACK CHART

Problem	Modification
I breathe before the corners.	Try to use the lift at the corners to breathe without any independent head movement. This will keep all your stroke actions moving in a unified line forward.
My stroke starts with the kick.	If your kick starts your stroke, then it is likely that the breathing will be out of time, and will reduce the productivity of the kick. You might find yourself having to kick again to regain forward motion. By starting the stroke sequence with the arm stroke, position your body to kick most effectively.
My glide doesn't last as long as the other three steps combined.	Make sure you are kicking with flexed feet, and that your body position during the glide is "downhill". Practice doing the first three steps quickly, so you gather momentum to glide better.

74 Glide Length, Glide Speed

THE PURPOSE OF THIS DRILL
- Developing a productive glide
- Recognizing when to start the next stroke
- Using momentum to rest and benefit the next stroke

HOW TO DO THIS DRILL
Step 1: Push off the wall for the breaststroke, arms extended, hand forming the point of an arrow, looking at the bottom of the pool. Watching the bottom of the pool, glide until you come to a complete stop. Stand and make note of your distance.

210

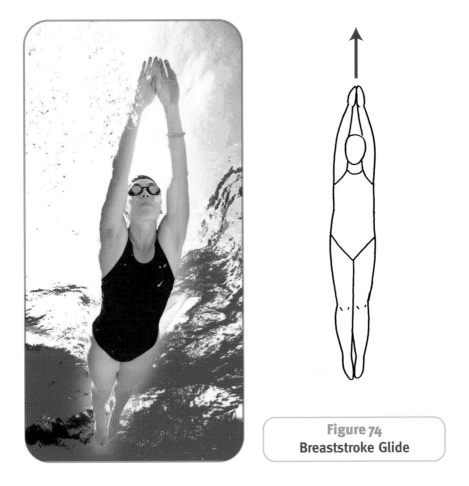

Figure 74
Breaststroke Glide

Step 2: Again, push off the wall for the breaststroke. Watch the bottom of the pool, and this time glide until you start to slow down. Stand and compare your distance to your first glide. Notice that there is not much difference in the distance you have travelled. By gliding until you completely stop, you use much more time to travel a little more distance.

Step 3: Try the comparison again with a glide plus a stroke. First push off and glide until you stop. At that point do one complete breaststroke. Stand and make note of your distance. Again push off the wall. This time, just as you start to slow down, do one complete

stroke. Stand and compare your distance to your first glide and stroke. Notice that you have travelled the same distance, or even farther with the second method. By bringing some of the momentum with you into the stroke, the length of your glide may be shorter, but you travel father overall.

Step 4: Try the drill again several times. Focus on finding the exact point where you maximize the length of your glide without sacrificing speed or momentum.

DRILL FEEDBACK CHART

Problem	Modification
A longer glide seems to be easier.	Looking at it in terms of swimming a few strokes, it probably is easier. However, if you have to keep swimming for more than a very short distance, it will be require less swimming time to cover that distance if you rest during your glide, but carry some momentum into the next stroke. In this way, your effort is reduced because you don't have to start the next stroke from a still position.
I am not gliding very far before I float to the surface.	Make sure you are looking at the bottom of the pool during your glide. Also make sure that your fingertips are pointed forward, not upward. Push off with force.
I am not producing very much momentum with my kick.	Make sure you are using flexed feet to kick, and that your kick is following a rounded path. Also make sure you are achieving a "downhill" streamlined position to glide.

Thread the Needle

75

THE PURPOSE OF THIS DRILL
- Achieving coordinated forward motion
- Maximizing streamline and momentum
- Learning to rest during the glide instead of the recovery

HOW TO DO THIS DRILL
Step 1: Push off the wall preparing to do the breaststroke. Focus on your body position while gliding forward. It should be long, narrow and streamlined. Your head should be tight between your elbows, and you should be looking at the bottom of the pool. Your legs should be extended and together, toes pointed. This is the position you should strive for with each glide. It is the position that makes the smallest hole in the water. First made with your fingertips, it is the same hole passed through by your forearms, elbows and head, shoulders, chest, hips, legs and finally your feet.

Step 2: Begin to swim breaststroke, focusing on achieving a long, narrow streamlined glide after each kick. Try to get back to the streamlined position as quickly as possible after each stroke. Notice that you don't have to wait until you have fully achieved streamline to make your small hole in the water. Begin as you recover, shooting your hands forward to a long narrow point before your feet have finished kicking.

Step 3: Pretend the small hole that you pass through in your glide position is right in front of you as you transition into recovery. Pretend you have to pass through it like your were thread passing through the eye of a needle. Create a narrow leading edge with your hands. Keep your chin low and shoot your elbows forward, with your forearms close together as your chest and head drop down.

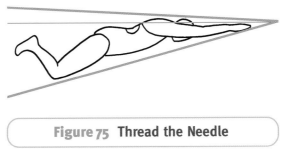

Figure 75 Thread the Needle

Step 4: Maintain a firm spine as you thread the needle through recovery, achieving streamline the instant your feet come together and through the eye of the needle at the end of the kick. Notice that the recovery in breaststroke works best as an active part of the stroke action, unlike in other strokes where a swimmer can use recovery to rest. In breaststroke it is after the recovery, during the streamlined glide that the swimmer has a moment to rest.

Step 5: Continue practicing, threading the needle with each stroke, from the beginning of the recovery through to the end of the kick.

DRILL FEEDBACK CHART

Problem	Modification
My head is not in streamline until after the kick.	Use a low chin breathing position, with a quick arm recovery, so your head will drop between your elbows as soon as they are straight, threading the needle with your arms and head, as you achieve a full upper body streamline during the kick rather than after it.
My hands begin recovery out of the water.	This is fine. It means you have produced major lift through the arm stroke. It is important to make a smooth transition from the breathing position into the streamlined glide. Shrug your shoulders up then down and forward, and, shoot to streamline. Doing so should aim your arms "downhill" into the water, and lead the rest of your body into the glide position.
My hips are low at the end of recovery.	Make sure you are looking at the bottom of the pool and not forward. Looking forward at this point in the stroke will cause your hips to drop. Also, make sure that you maintain a firm spine and drop your chest down before your arms reach streamline. This will shift your weight forward.

DRILLS FOR

BUTTERFLY

BODY POSITION DRILLS

The best butterfliers combine grace and power in what seems like effortless forward motion. The primary point of technique that these butterfliers share is good body position. While the line of the stroke is characterized by a wave or rocking motion, it is a stable, high hip floating position that is key to a good stroke. This position balances the stroke, and integrates the actions of both the upper and lower body. Often, swimmers attempt to achieve the rocking effect of the butterfly by folding both forward and back at the hips. Doing so eliminates core stability, lowers the hips, and eliminates balance in the stroke. It can also lead to back pain. The goal of the following drills for the butterfly body position is to develop a firm core, high hip body position for better balance and integration of butterfly actions.

Taking a Bow

76

THE PURPOSE OF THIS DRILL
* Learning to stabilize motion using the abdominals
* Isolating upper body motion
* Using abdominal muscles to maintain a straight spine

HOW TO DO THIS DRILL
Step 1: Stand with your head, back and legs against a wall, arms at your sides. Notice at the small of your back, you can fit your hand between the wall and your back. To achieve a truly firm core, you must straighten your spine, and eliminate this space at the small of your back. To do so, pull your belly button back toward your spine, and press the small of your back into the wall. Notice that to do this, you contract your abdominal muscles.

Step 2: Maintaining your spine straight with contracted abdominals, press your chest forward away from the wall about six inches, as if taking a bow. Keep your hips and lower body firmly against the wall,

controlling the speed of the movement. Hold this position for five seconds, stabilizing your position with your abdominal muscles.

Step 3: Keeping your core firm, return your back to the wall. Check to see if you have maintained a straight spine by trying to fit your hand between the wall and the small of your back. Repeat the bow, actively using your

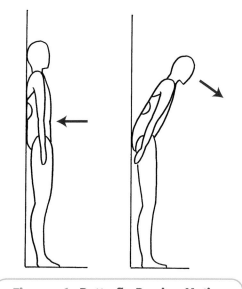

Figure 76   Butterfly Bowing Motion

abdominal muscles to maintain a straight spine, and to stabilize your upper body throughout the bow. Notice that your hips remain stable through the entire range of motion.

Step 4: Now, try the same bowing action without the support of the wall. Maintain a straight spine. Keep your hips stable. Use your abdominal muscles to control the movement of your upper body, while your lower body remains still.

DRILL FEEDBACK CHART

Problem	Modification
It is much harder without the support of the wall.	Yes, harder than it would seem. Start by rocking your pelvis forward a bit. Then, engage your abdominal muscles to stabilize your upper body in both directions during this motion.
I can't keep my hips stable without the wall.	Make sure your head is aligned with your straight spine. Also make sure you are not bowing too deeply. Try starting with only a three-inch bow, focusing on moving your upper body only. Contract your abdominal muscles going into the bow to stabilize your movement.
I am using my back muscles.	It is tempting to use the muscles of the back. As land animals, we spend most of our time vertical, and we are used to depending on the muscles of the back for stability and balance. In the water, however, we move horizontally, and to achieve the best stabilization and balance, we must use primarily the muscles of the abdomen.

77 Weight Shifting

THE PURPOSE OF THIS DRILL
- Feeling both natural and "downhill" body positions
- Learning to shift weight forward
- Developing effective core tension and stability

HOW TO DO THIS DRILL

Step 1: Lay in the water, arms at your sides. Look at the bottom of the pool. Feel your natural floating position. In butterfly, you have to learn to actively change from your natural float to a "downhill" position. You must learn to shift your weight forward so your chest is lower than your hips, during every single stroke. To do this, you must maintain a firm core and upper body, from your neck through to your hips.

Step 2: Holding your core firm, press your chest down into the water. Allow your chest to be lower than your hips. Feel your weight shift forward. Now release your chest press and allow your body to return to its natural float.

Step 3: Again press your chest down into the water, so you achieve a "downhill" float. Maintaining your firm core, release your chest press and return to your natural float. Repeat several times in a row, maintaining a firm core in both directions in a gentle, rhythmic action. Notice that as your press and release your chest, your hips remain stable in the water. This is the essential position of the butterfly. All other actions depend on this high hip floatation that shifts between the natural and "downhill" upper body positions.

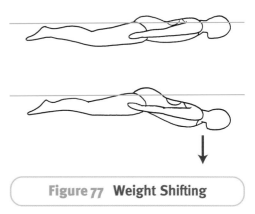

Figure 77 **Weight Shifting**

Step 4: Now push off the wall, with your arms extended over your head. Feel your natural float, then, maintaining your firm core, change it, shifting your weight forward by pressing your chest into the water. Release and do it again, maintaining high hips.

Step 5: Repeat the upper body shift of weight several times, from natural to "downhill" and back again. Feel the gentle wave produced by alternating your floating position. Feel your hips remain stable.

DRILL FEEDBACK CHART

Problem	Modification
I can't breathe.	This drill is not meant to be done for an extended time. Take a big breath before you start, then stand up when you need more air. Start again with a new breath.
When I press my chest down, my legs sink.	Hold your core firm. Avoid folding at the hips or waist. Just press your chest down a few inches, just enough so your weight shifts forward. When your chest is the lowest point of your float, then release it. Switch your weight about once every two seconds in a rhythmic motion.
This hurts my back.	It is important that you hold your core firm in both directions, or your back will take a lot of stress. Also, when you return to your natural float, don't force it. Simply allow your body to resume its natural position. If it continues to hurt you, just don't do it.

KICK DRILLS

The butterfly uses the dolphin kick, where the legs move up and down simultaneously resembling the action of a dolphin's tail. In fact it is more than a leg motion. It is an entire body motion. It is more accurately called simply the dolphin. Done right it is one of the most powerful movements in swimming. The dolphin uses a whip-like motion that starts high in the body, and moves down through the trunk, hips and legs, and ends up with the feet snapping down and up again. The dolphin provides rhythm and balance to the other actions of the stroke, but above all it adds power. A good dolphin makes the butterfly much easier, and much more sustainable. The goal of the following kicking drills for butterfly is to develop an effective, rhythmic and effective dolphin action that benefits the rest of the stroke.

Ribbon Writing

78

THE PURPOSE OF THIS DRILL
- Understanding the fluid nature of the dolphin
- Generating power high in the body
- Learning to transfer power to the feet

HOW TO DO THIS DRILL
Step 1: Cut a piece of wide ribbon to a length of about fifteen inches. Stand in chest deep water, and hold the ribbon in one hand, with that arm outstretched in front of you, under the water. Begin to sweep your arm down about twelve to fifteen inches, and back up, keeping your hand from breaking the surface of the water at its highest point. Sweep your outstretched arm down and up rhythmically at a rate that the ribbon begins to follow the movement of your arm.

Step 2: Notice how the ribbon creates a sort of "S" shape as it flows through the water. Notice too, that although the arm holding the ribbon is initiating the movement, it is the free end of the ribbon that is moving more quickly. This is the essence of the

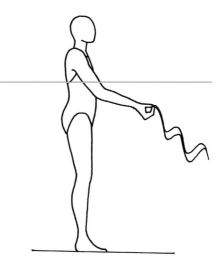

Figure 78   Observing fluid motion

223

dolphin action. While the action is initiated high in the body, it is the feet that exhibit the most motion.

Step 3: Continue making an "S" or wave with the ribbon, sweeping your outstretched arm down and up through the water. Watch the free end of the ribbon react to the motion of your sweeping arm. Now, without slowing the rhythm of your arm movement, bend at the elbow, and attempt to continue the ribbon's movement using just the lower portion of your arm, from your elbow to your hand. Notice that the wave action of the ribbon diminishes significantly. This is what happens when a swimmer over-bends at the knees doing dolphin.

Step 4: Re-establish your full arm motion, and watch the ribbon again flow through a continuous "S" shape. Without bending radically at the elbow or wrist, try to make your arm move fluidly through the water, as if your arm was part of the ribbon. This is how a good dolphin works, fluidly, gathering the force of the motion started high in the body and transferring it downward to the feet.

DRILL FEEDBACK CHART

Problem	Modification
My ribbon doesn't make a wave.	Try to make the down and up motion with your arm continuous. Don't slow down as you change directions. Use a smooth, sweeping motion, initiated from the shoulder, rather than from the hand.
My ribbon makes a "Z" not an "S".	Try to switch directions more smoothly. Fluidly and rhythmically sweep the ribbon back and forth, and avoid any jerking movements.
The free end of my ribbon is not a part of the wave.	Sweep your arm a little faster, and use more depth. Let your arm be long and relaxed until the entire length of the ribbon flows through the wave.

Deep to Shallow Dolphin

79

THE PURPOSE OF THIS DRILL
* Practicing full-body dolphin
* Experiencing the forward line of the dolphin
* Achieving a compact dolphin wave

HOW TO DO THIS DRILL

Step 1: At a depth of about six feet, lay face down in the water, arms at your sides. With a firm core and straight spine, bow forward, maintaining a stable hip position. Feel your head lead your body downward toward the bottom of the pool. Allow your legs and feet to follow. Watch your descent carefully, and before reaching the bottom of the pool, come out of your bow by raising your upper body, allowing your legs and feet to follow the same path. As your head rises, your feet should snap downward. At the top of your ascent, your face will clear the water, and you can grab a new breath. Then bow forward again. Repeat this extreme dolphin action several times, following a forward path that is at least four feet of deep.

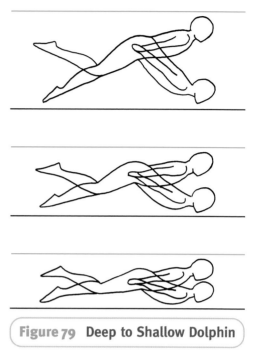

Step 2: Now move to shallower water, perhaps three feet deep. Lay face down in the water, arms at your sides. With your spine straight and core firm, bow forward, maintaining a high hip position. Feel your body descend downward. Feel your legs and feet follow the same line of descent.

Figure 79 Deep to Shallow Dolphin

Raise your upper body out of your bow before reaching the bottom of the pool. Your legs and feet should follow the same path. As your head rises, feel your feet snap downward. Breathe, then bow forward again, repeating the wave-like dolphin action that passes through a depth of only one and a half feet.

Step 3: Now you have to pretend that you are in water that is only one foot deep. Lay face down in the water, arms at your sides with a straight spine and firm core. Bow forward, maintaining your high hip position. Allow your upper body to descend. Feel your hips, legs and feet react. Quickly, before reaching the bottom of the one-foot deep water, raise your upper body out of the bow. Feel your legs and feet follow quickly. As you head rises, feel your feet snap quickly downward. Breathe then bow forward again, repeating a very compact, yet effective forward wave-like dolphin action that is only a few inches deep.

DRILL FEEDBACK CHART

Problem	Modification
After I breathe, I can't achieve another dolphin.	Be sure you are maintaining a straight spine through your neck, and that you are not raising your chin to breathe. Without this firm spine line, you head will be leading you in a different direction than your body is trying to go.
I am not moving forward.	Make sure you are not simply folding in half at the waist, but simply bowing your upper body forward. If you allow your legs to sink as your chest is descending, your forward motion will be reduced. Your legs must follow the same line that your upper body has travelled.
I can only make a slight wave in the shallowest water.	Yes, but it is there. Practice condensing all of the power of the dolphin into those few inches of depth. An effective dolphin that is compact uses a shorter path to the other end of the pool.

80 Dolphin Dives

THE PURPOSE OF THIS DRILL
- Understanding the full-body action of the dolphin
- Experiencing the line of the dolphin
- Feeling the transfer of power to the feet

HOW TO DO THIS DRILL
Step 1: Stand in water about hip deep, arms firmly at your sides. Using the muscles of your core, achieve a straight spine from your hips through your neck. Keeping your hips firm, bow forward about twelve inches. At the same time, bend your knees slightly, preparing to jump off the bottom of the pool.

Step 2: Maintaining your bowed position, jump off the bottom with force. As your body rises into the air, bow forward more. Notice that by doing so, the upward force of your jump changes to follow your head forward.

Step 3: At the highest point in your jump, bow forward even more. As you begin to descend, notice that instead of landing back on your feet, you are going to re-enter the water head first. By shifting the position of your upper body, you have changed the line of your jump from a simple up and down path, that landed in the same place it started, to a line that travels forward. By bowing forward, you go up out of the water, forward over the water, and then down into the water. At the point your head enters the water, your hips should actually be higher than your head.

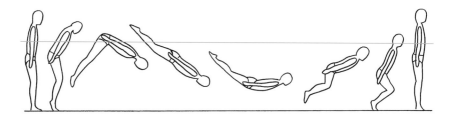

Figure 80 Dolphin Dives

Step 4: You should be aiming head first toward the bottom of the pool, with quite a bit of speed. Your upper body, hips, legs and feet should be following the same line. KEEP YOUR EYES OPEN, and well before you reach the bottom of the pool, raise your upper body out of your bow, again changing the line of your jump.

Step 5: As the upper body rises toward the surface, feel your hips, legs and feet react to the change of direction. As your face approaches the surface of water, feel your feet snap down into the water. Your whole body has just travelled through an exaggerated dolphin movement. Draw your legs up under you as you resume a standing position.

Step 6: Try it several times. Maintaining a straight spine, actively bow forward and jump up with force. Feel your head and upper body lead you through the wave of the dolphin as you bow forward more. Feel your body travel up, over, then down into the water, head first. Then as you come out of your bow, feel your feet snap down. Stand. Practice several times, until you can do several dolphin dives smoothly in a row without pausing between them.

DRILL FEEDBACK CHART

Problem	Modification
I am landing on my belly.	Jump up with more force, and bow forward more as you feel the upward force of your jump. Bow even more at your highest point so you are aiming more downward than forward as you descend from your jump.
I am not aiming toward the bottom of the pool.	Remember, your body will follow your head. Make sure your spine is straight and firm from your hips through your neck. If you raise your chin, bending at the neck, and breaking your straight spine line, the downward line your upper body is travelling at this point will be compromised. If your head is raised, your body won't aim toward the bottom of the pool.
My feet don't snap down before I stand.	Maintain your firm core. Allow your legs and feet to travel the same line that your upper body has travelled. They will still be moving downward for a moment when your upper body has shifted out of the bow. It is when your hips and legs finally change directions, and begin their path upward that your feet will snap downward. Draw your legs under you only after that point.

 Vertical Dolphin

THE PURPOSE OF THIS DRILL
- Developing a productive dolphin
- Practicing a continuous kick
- Using a fluid, full-body dolphin

HOW TO DO THIS DRILL

Step 1: In water, at least as deep as you are tall, get into a vertical position. Engage your core. With your hands extended out from your sides, begin a gentle sculling action, tracing side-to-side underwater figure eights with your hands, to keep your head above water.

Step 2: Holding your legs together, but relaxed, begin a gentle dolphin action by bowing down and up, allowing your legs and feet to sweep forward and back in reaction. With your ankles relaxed, allow your feet to snap forward as you come out of your bow. Begin another bow immediately, and repeat this motion several times in a row creating a rhythmic wave. Your feet should be sweeping across about fifteen inches of water.

Step 3: As your extended legs move simultaneously in a sweeping motion forward and back in the water, think about the movement of a dolphin's tail. Where does it begin? In fact, the dolphin uses the entire length of its body to produce motion. Pretend you have the tail of a dolphin, that your trunk and legs are part of the movement. You have no waist or hips, and no knees to bend. Your movement is fluid and your entire body works to sweep the water in a wave-like movement. Continue your dolphin until it seems there is no beginning or end to the motion.

Step 4: Once you have achieved a fluid dolphin action, stop the sculling action with your hands. Position your hands: left hand on right shoulder and right hand on left shoulder. Continue your vertical dolphin keeping your head above water. Maintain for 30 seconds. Rest, and then practice again.

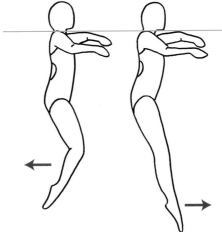

Figure 81 Vertical Dolphin

DRILL FEEDBACK CHART

Problem	Modification
I am sinking.	Make sure you are sweeping the water back and forth and not trying to kick down and up, bending a lot at the hips and knees.
I feel it in my stomach.	Good! This shows you are using more than your legs for your dolphin action.
I get tired too quickly to notice a floppy kicking motion.	Maintain a firm core, and allow your lower body to follow the movement of your upper body. Remember that the best dolphin is compact; so try to produce an effective wave in a small amount of space.

Back Dolphin

82

THE PURPOSE OF THIS DRILL
- Using the abdominal muscles for dolphin
- Gathering power for lower body movement
- Avoiding over bending at the knees

HOW TO DO THIS DRILL

Step 1: Push off the wall on your back, arms at your sides. Begin a gentle dolphin action, high in your body and allow it to gather force as it travels down to your feet.

Step 2: Try to kick the water upward enough to make a small boiling effect over your feet. Drop your legs down, then kick up again. Create a rhythmic up and down motion with your legs that extends about 15 inches deep. Use the entire length of your legs and your trunk for dolphin on your back.

Step 3: Your head should be almost still as your core and legs move. Try to keep your head from bouncing so your face submerges. Also, watch your knees to make sure they are not coming out of the water too much, or they will produce a wave of water over your face. Sweep the water upward and downward, rather than closer to you and then father away. Practice several times.

Step 4: Once you have achieved a fluid dolphin action on your back, and forward motion, try it with your arms extended over your head. Produce a smooth, rhythmic dolphin action that starts high in your body and gathers force down to your feet. Feel how your abdominal muscles are engaged. Sweep the water up and down, producing forward motion, while your face stays above water. Practice several times.

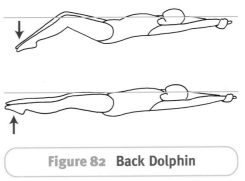

Figure 82 Back Dolphin

DRILL FEEDBACK CHART

Problem	Modification
I can't keep my face above water.	Avoid moving your upper body back beyond your natural floating position. Doing so will prevent the power of the dolphin from flowing down to your feet.
I am not moving.	Keep practicing. You don't have to do a large kick to move. Try a dolphin only a few inches deep at first. Kick upward with more force.
I am feeling it in my calves.	This indicates that you are using only your lower legs, from your knees down, to kick. Try initiating the action from your core. You should be feeling it in your abdominal muscles.

ARM STROKE DRILLS

The path of the butterfly underwater arm stroke is similar to the freestyle arm stroke, only it is done with both arms simultaneously. It is an extremely powerful arm stroke, and for a short distance can rival the freestyle in speed. However, because it is just not as sustainable as the freestyle, it is even more important to practice the most economic butterfly arm stroke possible, so that butterfly can be done well for longer. The goal of the following arm stroke drills for butterfly is to develop a productive arm stroke that maximizes power and minimizes effort.

Pitch to Press

THE PURPOSE OF THIS DRILL
* Feeling the path of the butterfly arm stroke
* Learning to press back, and not down
* Using correct hand pitch to maintain pressure on the water

HOW TO DO THIS DRILL

Step 1: Stand in waist deep water. Keeping your feet firmly on the bottom of the pool, bow forward so your face is in the water. Look at the bottom of the pool. Extend your arms forward on the surface of the water slightly wider than your shoulders. With your palms down, position your thumbs slightly lower than your pinkies.

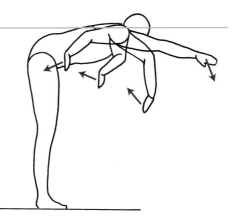

Figure 83 Pitch Hands to Press on the Water

Step 2: Stretch your arms forward, so that your elbows are locked. This should extend your reach, and position your hands slightly farther apart. As your hands achieve their longest reach, bend at the wrists slightly so your palms and fingertips are lower than your wrists and pitched outward. Sweep your palms around so you are pressing back on the water, not pushing down. Allow your forearms to follow your hands, but keep your elbows high and firm. Watch your hands as they pass your face, pressing back and sweeping slightly inward, so they are closer together than their starting point.

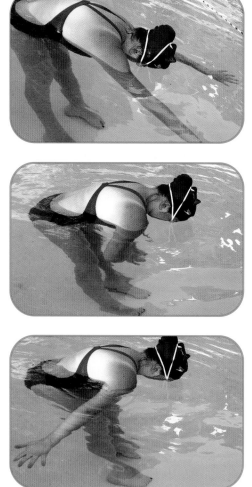

Step 3: As your hands continue pressing back and pass your shoulders, they should also sweep by your elbows. Adjust the position of your hands so they maintain firm pressure on the water. As your hands pass under your belly they should be at their closest point together, closer together than your elbows. Again adjust the pitch of your hands so they can continue pressing back. The arm stroke finishes with the hands pressing back quickly, until the arms are straight and outside each hip.

Step 4: Take a breath and return your hands and head to the starting position, slightly wider than your shoulders. Repeat the arm stroke, stretching forward until your elbows lock, then sweeping your palms around and positioning them to press back on the water, with your elbows high. As your hands press back towards your belly and get closer together, change your hand pitch again to sweep quickly back, until your arms are straight and out from your hips.

Step 5: Continue performing the butterfly arm stroke several times. Constantly reposition your hands so they press back on the water and not down. Practice until you can perform several quick arm strokes in a row, producing enough pressure back on the water so it is difficult to maintain your footing on the bottom of the pool.

DRILL FEEDBACK CHART

Problem	Modification
My hand press down then up.	Change the pitch of your hands to press back on the water from the beginning through to the end of the stroke in order to move forward. Otherwise your efforts will be used to move up and down.
My hands are almost touching at their closest point.	Correctly positioned, your thumbs might be fairly close, but the fingertips of each hand should be pointing at the bottom of the pool. Make sure that your elbows are not leading your stroke. They should stay high and firm throughout the stroke.
It feels like a large sculling action.	Exactly! You change the pitch of your hand to maintain pressure on the water. Press out with your thumbs down, and in with your thumbs up.

237

84 Sweeping Question Marks

THE PURPOSE OF THIS DRILL
- Feeling the path of the butterfly arm stroke
- Sweeping wide to narrow
- Sweeping deep to shallow

HOW TO DO THIS DRILL

Step 1: Push off the wall face down in the water, arms extended in front of your shoulders. Achieve a "downhill", and high hip float. Look at the bottom of the pool. While still gliding forward, perform a single butterfly stroke with both arms simultaneously moving in a wide to narrow line. Stretch forward, sweep out and around, then inward toward your belly. Finish by pressing back quickly past your waist. Notice that the lines you have traced with your arm stroke resemble two question marks, one the mirror image of the other floating flat on the surface of the water. Stand and breathe.

Step 2: Return to the wall, and push off for the butterfly again. Float "downhill" with high hips. Look at the bottom of the pool. Using the momentum of your push off, again do one butterfly stroke tracing a deep to shallow line. Stretch forward, sweep down and around, then upward under your belly. Finish by pressing back quickly past your waist. Notice that the lines you have traced with your arm stroke resemble two question marks, one the mirror image of the other floating perpendicular to the surface of the water. Stand and breathe.

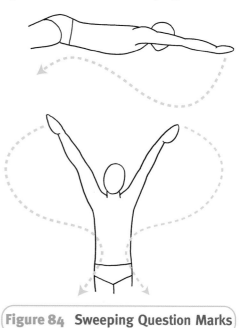

Figure 84 Sweeping Question Marks

238

Step 3: Return to the wall, and push off for the butterfly once again. Look at the bottom of the pool and achieve a high hip "downhill" floating position. With the forward motion of your glide, do a butterfly stroke tracing a wide to narrow, and deep to  shallow path at the same time. Stretch forward, sweep out and down, around, then inward and upward under your belly. Finish by pressing back quickly past your waist. Notice that the lines you have traced with your arm stroke resemble question marks floating diagonally in the water, one the mirror image of the other.

Step 4: Stand and breathe. Continue to practice the path of the butterfly arm stroke tracing deep to shallow and wide to narrow question marks at the same time.

DRILL FEEDBACK CHART

Problem	Modification
My arm stroke goes straight back, not like question marks.	You will be able to achieve a longer, more productive stroke if you use the sweeping question mark arm stroke. You will be able to use fewer strokes, and therefore less energy to cross the pool.
My arms are shallow the whole way.	Make sure you are holding your elbows firm to start the stroke. Move your hands first, and allow them to pass under your elbows to achieve depth.
My arms are deep the whole way.	To be strongest in the middle of the arm stroke, allow your hands to sweep closer under your belly.

85 One-arm Butterfly

THE PURPOSE OF THIS DRILL
- Feeling the rhythm of the butterfly arm stroke
- Practicing the path of the arm stroke
- Pressing back on the water

HOW TO DO THIS DRILL

Step 1: Push off the wall face down in the water, arms extended in front of your shoulders. Achieve a "downhill", high hip float. With your right hand remaining in the extended position, perform a single butterfly stroke with your left arm. Stretch forward, sweep out and around, then inward under your belly. Finish by pressing back quickly past your waist. Breathe toward the moving arm, and do an over-the-water, freestyle-like recovery.

Step 2: Do another stroke with the same arm, accompanied by a light dolphin action. When your hand stretches forward, your chest should be low in the water. Your feet should snap down as you first press on the water. Then, when your hand presses back to the finish, your chest should be high, as your feet should snap down again. Remember that the dolphin action should be generated high in the body, without excessive knee bend. Repeat the one arm butterfly several times, tracing the wide to narrow, and, deep to shallow line of the stroke. Maintain pressure back on the water, and use two dolphins with each arm

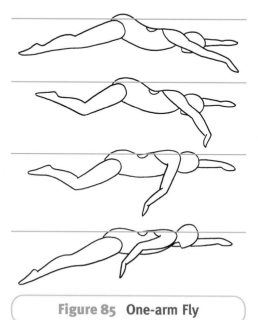

Figure 85 One-arm Fly

stroke. The first dolphin propels you into the beginning of the arm stroke. The second dolphin assists the fast finish of the arm stroke.

Step 3: Continue practicing your one-arm butterfly arm stroke, accompanied by a rhythmic light dolphin action. Focus on accelerating your stroke to the rear. Maintain a hand pitch that you can constantly press back on the water, not down or up. From front to back, stretch forward, sweep out and around, inward under your belly, wide to narrow, and, deep to shallow. Finish by pressing back quickly. Breathe. Recover. Repeat to the far end of the pool.

Step 4: After resting, push off the wall and leave your left arm extended. Perform the one-arm butterfly with your right arm. Match your light dolphin to accompany the start and the finish of the stroke. Accelerate the stroke toward the rear. Continue to the far end of the pool.

Step 5: Practice the one-arm butterfly for several lengths of the pool. Keep your hips high and time the kick to match the beginning and end of your arm stroke. Feel your dolphin move through your body and assist you in catching water at the beginning of the stroke. Feel your dolphin assist you again to finish the stroke with speed.

241

DRILL FEEDBACK CHART

Problem	Modification
I am leaning to one side a bit.	That is okay. The more forward momentum you produce, the less noticeable this will be. Focus on accelerating your arm to the back of the stroke, and maintaining pressure back on the water the whole time.
My hands are aimed inward at the start of the stroke.	Starting in the correct position is important in order to begin the stroke from a position of power. Your hands should enter at shoulder width apart or even wider, but not closer. Your fingertips should be pointing forward, and a bit outward. In this position, be sure to lock your elbows and stretch forward to the far end of the pool.
I am not accelerating at the end of the stroke.	Make sure you are starting the stroke by moving your hands, not your elbows. If your elbows move first, you will not be in position to accelerate your hands to the end of the stroke.

86 Left Arm, Right Arm, Both Arms

THE PURPOSE OF THIS DRILL
- Feeling the line of the stroke
- Practicing accelerating to the back of the stroke
- Experiencing butterfly rhythm

HOW TO DO THIS DRILL
Step 1: Push off the wall face down in the water, arms extended in front of your shoulders. Achieve a "downhill" float. Maintain high hips. With your right hand remaining in the extended position,

perform a single butterfly stroke with your left arm, accompanied by a rhythmic light dolphin action. Focus on accelerating your stroke to the rear. Breathe toward the moving arm, and recover, like freestyle, over the water.

Step 2: As your left arm reaches the front and engages the water, your feet should snap down. As they do, begin stroking with your right arm, leaving your left arm extended in front of you. Accelerate to the back again. Allow your feet to snap down again as you finish the stroke. Recover.

Step 3: Now, with both arms extended in front, perform a butterfly arm

Figure 86
Left Arm, Right Arm, Both Arms

stroke with both arms. Bow forward and stretch your elbows to the locked position as your feet snap down. Press out and sweep around, positioning your hands to press back. Accelerate your arm stroke as your hands move past your belly, closer together than your elbows. Finish by pressing quickly back toward your hips as your feet snap down again. Return your arms over the surface of the water to the starting position in front.

Step 4: Repeat the sequence. Left arm, right arm, both arms, maintaining a light rhythmic dolphin that matches the beginning and the end of the stroke. Maintain pressure back on the water, and an accelerating stroke. Continue to the far end of the pool. Rest, then

243

practice again until you are moving comfortably and rhythmically through the water.

DRILL FEEDBACK CHART

Problem	Modification
My arms sink down in front.	Remember to stretch your arm forward when you enter. Reach toward the far end of the pool, then sweep around and press back on the water, not down.
I don't know when to breathe on the stroke with both arms.	For this drill, don't breathe on the double arm stroke. Focus on the path of the stroke, maintaining constant pressure back on the water, and accelerating your stroke toward your hips. You can breathe on the one-arm strokes.
My arms get stuck at the rear on the two-arm stroke.	Make sure your hands are the first part of your arm to move. Hold your elbows firm. If your elbows move first, your hands won't clear the water at the rear.

The Round Off

87

THE PURPOSE OF THIS DRILL
- Pressing outward the end of the stroke
- Practicing a quick finish of the stroke
- Learning to release the water in back

HOW TO DO THIS DRILL

Step 1: Push off the wall face down in the water, arms extended in front of your shoulders. Achieve a "downhill" float. Do several dolphins in a row, beginning each high in your body and snapping downward to your feet. On the sixth dolphin, start your arm stroke, bowing forward as your reach, then sweeping around and back, closer under your belly.

Step 2: As your hands accelerate toward the end of your stroke, pitch your palms slightly outward. Press back and outward from your body in a fast finish as your feet snap down again. Your hands should clear the water between your waist and your hips, several inches away from your body. Return them to the front, extended and slightly wider than your shoulders.

Step 3: Do another arm stroke, tracing question marks. As your hands approach their closest point under your belly, press them back with speed, and outward like a "J". Your hands should release the water and rise easily up through the surface with your pinkies up.

Step 4: Return them to the front, again. Stretch forward and engage your palms. Sweep around and press back against the water. Feel your hands get closer together under your belly, then accelerate into your fast finish, rounding off at

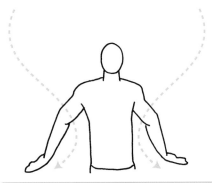

Figure 87
Round off at the End of the Stroke

245

the rear of the stroke in a "J" shape out from your body. Feel your hands rise easily up through the surface of the water with no resistance. Use their momentum to return to the front. Repeat several times, accelerating to the rounded off finish of your stroke.

DRILL FEEDBACK CHART

Problem	Modification
My arm stroke makes more forward motion when I push straight back.	With the round off, your hands are actually travelling the same distance, but not so far back along your body. When the arm stroke goes straight back, the path back to the front takes longer, so the kicks have to be spaced farther apart in order to occur at the most beneficial points in the stroke. This can produce "dead space" or loss of momentum.
My hands come out of the water, palms up.	Make sure you are not lifting the water up at the end of the "J". Position your hands so you are pushing it back and outward. Your pinkie should leave the water first.
This makes my stroke short.	Again, the distance of the actual stroke path is the same, it just curves outward more. Your stroke turn-over will be quicker, because the recovery path is shorter. This allows you to spend more time with your hands pressing against the water, and less time with them in the air.

RECOVERY DRILLS

The butterfly uses a simultaneous arm recovery over the surface of the water. It is this characteristic spread wing position that makes the butterfly such a favorite photo opportunity. It is important to use a relaxed recovery, however, variations in flexibility make each swimmer's butterfly recovery slightly unique. In general, the recovery is close to the water, as the arms swing around wide from back to front. When the arms pass the shoulders, they realign to aim forward. The goal of the following recovery drills for the butterfly is to achieve a relaxed, direct, and well-aligned recovery for a better butterfly.

Pinkies-up

88

THE PURPOSE OF THIS DRILL
- Learning to maintain a pinkie up position
- Feeling a relaxed recovery
- Creating an arch with your arms over the water

HOW TO DO THIS DRILL
Step 1: Standing in front of a mirror, bow forward so your upper body is horizontal. Beginning with your arms extended in front of you, do a butterfly arm stroke in the air, stretching forward then sweeping around, close through the middle, then quickly back and outward in a "J". Freeze after the "J". Notice that your pinkies are the high point of your hands.

Step 2: Maintaining your pinkie-up hand position, sweep your hand around and forward through recovery, toward the starting position. Your arms and hands should be relaxed. Notice the arch that your two arms make, with your head in the middle. Notice too that as you sweep to the widest wing span, in order to maintain a pinkie-up position, you have to lower your chest into the water.

247

Step 3: As your hands pass your shoulders, reach forward with your arms, still maintaining your pinkie-up position. Stretch forward, as if preparing to enter the water. Repeat the complete path of the butterfly arms several times looking in the mirror. Watch your hands maintain a pinkie-up position throughout their recovery. Feel your arms and hands relax as they swing around and forward.

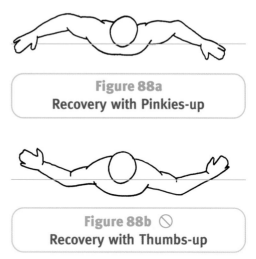

Figure 88a
Recovery with Pinkies-up

Figure 88b ⊘
Recovery with Thumbs-up

Step 4: Now try it in the water. Push off the wall face down in the water, arms extended in front of your shoulders. After several dolphins, start your arm stroke, reaching forward, then sweeping around and back, closer under your belly. Accelerate toward the end of your stroke, pitching your palms outward and back to finish in a quick "J" as your feet snap down again. Your hands should clear the

water, pinkies-up, several inches away from the sides of your body. Return them to the front in a relaxed wide arm swing, maintaining your pinkie-up position throughout the recovery. Extend your arms forward as your hands pass your shoulders, and enter the water slightly wider than your shoulders.

Step 5: Do another stroke, tracing a wide to narrow, and deep to shallow line, and accelerating to the rear. Round off the finish in a "J" , then slide your hands out of the water pinkies first. Recover pinkies-up, creating a relaxed arch over the water. Practice several times until you achieve a relaxed recovery with your pinkies-up the whole way.

DRILL FEEDBACK CHART

Problem	Modification
My elbows drag through the water during recovery.	This probably means your hands are recovering thumbs-up. In this position, your elbows are low and can drag through the water. Practice again, actively rotating your hands to the pinkie-up position and hold it throughout the recovery.
My hands start pinkie-up, but then turn over.	This means you are not relaxing during recovery, but instead pulling your hands forward. Try rotating your whole arm and shoulder forward to maintain the pinkie-up position. Try to initiate the recovery from higher in the arm.
My hands bump into each other in front.	As your hands pass your shoulders in the recovery, redirect your arms to reach forward rather than continuing the circular swing. It is important to align your stroke forward at the end of the recovery, and enter the water with your hands about shoulder width apart to avoid starting your next stroke from a position of weakness.

The Flop

THE PURPOSE OF THIS DRILL
- Using your chest and shoulders to recover
- Finishing the recovery in a "downhill" position
- Feeling a relaxed recovery

HOW TO DO THIS DRILL
Step 1: Push off the wall face for the butterfly. After several dolphins, start your arm stroke. Sweep your arms wide to narrow and deep to shallow, accelerating to the rear. Round off the end of the stroke and slide your hands out of the water pinkies first. Recover with a relaxed wide arm swing, maintaining your pinkie-up position. As your arms reach their widest position, your shoulders and head should be at the top of the arch of your recovery. Feel the swing of the recovery come from the shoulders and chest, rather than from the hands.

Step 2: When your hands pass your shoulders, roll your shoulders forward. Then as your arms realign to reach forward at the end of the recovery, drop your chest downward into the water. Do it again. Stroke and exit the water at the rear pinkies-up. Initiate your recovery from the shoulders and chest, maintaining a pinkie-up position. As your hands pass your shoulders, roll your shoulders forward. Drop your chest down into the water as your arms reach forward. It should feel like your arms are flopping forward effortlessly.

Step 3: Do several more strokes, focusing on your relaxed, pinkie-up recovery, powered from the chest and shoulders. At the midpoint in recovery, roll your shoulders forward, and drop your chest down as you realign your arms

Figure 89
Flop Your Recovering Arms Forward

forward with each recovery. Notice that doing so adds speed to the end of your recovery. Notice too that as your shoulder and chest action flops your arms automatically into their forward entry position, your body achieves a downhill floating position.

Step 4: Practice more, focusing on achieving a relaxed recovery from start to finish. Maintain a pinkie-up position each time. Flop your arms into their entry position using your shoulders and chest. Feel your body achieve a "downhill" position. Feel your arms landing in their forward entry position relaxed and aimed forward after each recovery.

DRILL FEEDBACK CHART

Problem	Modification
I do not end up in the "downhill" position.	Make sure that you are maintaining a straight spine from hips through to your neck. You should be looking at the bottom of the pool and not forward. Your hips should be high and stable as you flop forward.
My arms enter the water closer than my shoulders.	Realign your arms forward earlier in the recovery. Make sure your are reaching forward with your elbows straight, so your whole arm is aligned in the direction you are trying to go.
When I enter the water, my chest is the lowest part of my body.	Good. This means you will start your next stroke from a position of power.

90 Reaching to a "Y"

THE PURPOSE OF THIS DRILL
- Finishing recovery with your fingertips wider than your shoulders
- Aligning from the thumbs
- Positioning the hands to hold more water

HOW TO DO THIS DRILL
Step 1: Push off the wall preparing to do the butterfly, straight spine, high hips, arms extended. Establish your rhythm with several dolphins, then start your arm stroke, tracing question marks as you accelerate to the back. Round off your finish and recover pinkies-up. When your hands pass your shoulders, realign your arms to reach forward.

Step 2: At the end of the recovery, to prepare for the next stroke, drop your chest down, extend your arms forward, and push your elbows out straight. Point your thumbs to the far end of the pool. Notice that by doing so, your fingertips pitch outward. Do it again, actively aligning your recovery forward with your thumbs to finish your recovery. Feel your fingertips enter the water wider than your shoulders as you achieve the "downhill" position.

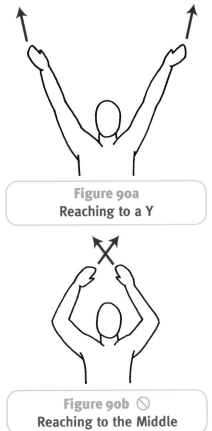

Figure 90a
Reaching to a Y

Figure 90b ⊘
Reaching to the Middle

Step 3: Do several more strokes, making a wide relaxed recovery, then redirect your arms to reach forward as your hands pass your shoulders. Drop your chest, press your elbows out straight, and align your reach to the far end of the pool with your thumbs. Fully extended, you should feel as if your arms form a "Y" on the surface of the water.

Step 4: Practice more, finishing each recovery by aligning your thumbs forward and achieving a "Y" entry position. Notice that by simply pointing with your thumbs, your arms enter aligned outside your shoulders. Notice too that from the "Y" position, you are able to take hold of the water better with your hands as you begin each new stroke.

DRILL FEEDBACK CHART

Problem	Modification
It feels too wide.	It is actually just your hands that are positioned wider than usual. Your arms are still aligned with your shoulders. This wide hand position enables you to catch and hold more water at the beginning of the stroke.
Entering this way my stroke misses the top part of the question mark.	There is very little forward motion produced by pressing outward. Entering in a "Y", positions your hands to immediately start a productive sweep around and back.
My fingertips are not wider than my shoulders.	Remember to push your elbows out straight. It is important to create a forward line from your shoulders, through your elbow, and all the way to your thumbs. If your elbows are not straight, the forward line of your stroke will be compromised.

BREATHING DRILLS

Breathing in the butterfly happens within the line of the stroke, so that the swimmer inhales when the upper body is naturally at its highest point, and finishes when the upper body regains its "downhill" position. Timed correctly, no independent head action is required to achieve a breath. The most economic breathing style is low on the water, facing forward. Regular, rhythmic breathing is important to achieving a sustainable stroke, but successful butterfliers use a variety of breathing patterns, from breathing every stroke, to breathing every third stroke. The goal of the following breathing drills for butterfly is to practice the correct timing of the breathing so it happens with the natural rhythm of the stroke.

91 Breathing Timing Drill

THE PURPOSE OF THIS DRILL
- Learning the timing of the butterfly breathing
- Achieving the inhale at the high point of the stroke
- Feeling the face return to the water before the hands

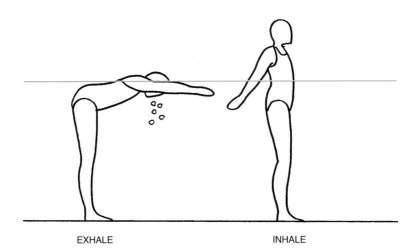

EXHALE   INHALE

Figure 91 Butterfly Breathing Timing

HOW TO DO THIS DRILL

Step 1: Stand in waist deep water. Keeping your feet firmly on the bottom of the pool, bow forward so your face is in the water. Look at the bottom of the pool. Extend your arms forward on the surface of the water, aligning your elbows and thumbs forward. Begin tracing the question mark line of your arm stroke. As your hands press back and accelerate to the end of the stroke, stand upright.

Step 2: Inhale as you achieve your full standing position, while your hands press quickly back and round off the finish of the stroke. As your hands leave the water, pinkies-up and move into the arch of the recovery, again bow forward so your body joins the forward line of the arms as they go over the water. Your face should submerge just before your hands enter the water in front.

Step 3: Begin another stroke, and stand as your hands transition to the fast finish. Inhale. Bow forward again as your arms recover, allowing your face to reach the water before your hands. Do several strokes, standing to inhale at the end of each one. As you move into the recovery and bow forward, notice that your head and arms move in unison towards the front. Your head should beat your arms to the water because it has a shorter distance to travel.

Step 4: Now try several strokes in a row. Bow forward to begin each stroke with your face in the water. Stand and inhale as your hands approach the back of the stroke. Bow forward again as your arms recover, so your face reaches the water an instant before your hands.

Step 5: Continue to practice, focusing on inhaling at the high point of your stroke. Allow your body position to determine when your breath begins and ends.

DRILL FEEDBACK CHART

Problem	Modification
My hands and face hit the water at the same time.	Try to get your face back to the water before your hands. Although they should be travelling in unison, your arms have a longer path to travel, so your face should reach the water first.
It seems like I am pressing down on the water, not back.	In this drill, since you are vertical, you will initially be pressing down. Try to pay attention to the timing of the breathing rather than the path of the stroke in this drill.
When my face hits the water, my hands are already stroking.	You might be breathing too late. Time the inhale to end as the arms are reaching forward toward the "Y".

Flying Dolphin Dives

92

THE PURPOSE OF THIS DRILL
* Learning the timing of the butterfly breathing
* Breathing within the line of the stroke
* Feeling the wave of the stroke

HOW TO DO THIS DRILL

Step 1: Stand in water that is hip deep, arms extended back and outside the hips, pinkies-up. Achieve a straight spine from your hips through your neck. Keeping your hips firm, bow forward about twelve inches while bending your knees slightly, preparing to jump off the bottom of the pool.

Step 2: Jump off the bottom with force. As your body rises into the air, bow forward more, and swing your arms around and forward like a butterfly recovery. Your arms should be finishing their recovery as your body begins to descend. As your face enters the water, your hips should actually be higher than your head, and your arms should be extended, and in the water, aiming downward toward the bottom of the pool.

Step 3: As your arms descend, your upper body, legs and feet should be following the same line, travelling up, over, then down into the water. Before you reach the bottom of the pool, sweep through the butterfly arm stroke, and raise your upper body out of your bow. Feel your legs and feet react to the change of direction. As your face rises to the surface of water, feel your feet snap down into

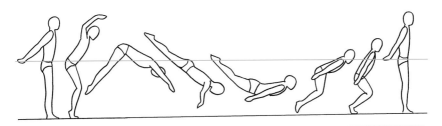

Figure 92 Flying Dolphin Dives

the water, as your hands reach the end of the stroke. Draw your legs up under you as you resume the standing position. Inhale.

Step 4: From the starting position, standing with your arms extended back and out from your body, begin another dolphin dive. Jump up and swing your arms into the recovery as you bow forward. Continue to bow forward so that by the high point of your jump, your hips are higher than your head, and your arms are pointing down toward the water. As

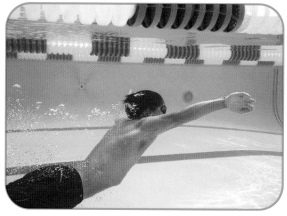

you descend into the water, trace the butterfly arm stroke as you come out of your bow. Finish your stroke as your face rises out of the water and your feet snap down. Inhale and resume your starting position.

Step 5: Perform several flying dolphin dives in a row, using the high point of each to inhale. Travel up, over, then down into the water with each one, maintaining a fluid rhythm from one to the next.

DRILL FEEDBACK CHART

Problem	Modification
I am landing flat on the water.	Bow forward more to start. Then bow forward even more as you jump up and swing of your arms around forward. Your legs should still be rising when your arms have finished their recovery, and are pointing with your head down toward the water.
My face doesn't clear the water until I stand.	As your arms finish the stroke and you come out of your bow, allow your legs to follow the same wave until your feet snap down. That will naturally lift your face to the surface before you stand up completely.
My face comes out of the water before my feet snap down.	This could means that you are raising your chin to breathe, rather than breathing within the wave of the dolphin dive. Hold your head position firm throughout the whole drill. Achieve your breathe at the high point of the dolphin dive, without changing your head position.

Eyes on the Water Butterfly   93

THE PURPOSE OF THIS DRILL
- Learning to maintain a stable head position
- Practicing looking down at the water while breathing
- Using the natural wave to the stroke to breathe

HOW TO DO THIS DRILL
Step 1: Push off the wall preparing to do the butterfly, straight spine, arms extended in front of you, looking down at the bottom of

the pool. Do several dolphins to establish your rhythm, then start your arm stroke. Sweep around and accelerate to the rear. Finish fast and feel your upper body rise. Breathe and begin the recovery. When your hands pass your shoulders and your chest drops down, allow your head to return to the water as you realign your arms to reach forward in a "Y".

Step 2: Continue into a second stroke. Look at the bottom of the pool. Maintain a firm spine, from your hips through to your neck. As your arms begin to sweep through the stroke, feel your upper body start to rise. As your arms accelerate to the finish, your feet should snap down again, propelling your face to the surface of the water. Inhale without changing your head position.

Step 3: Continue into the recovery. Your head should be moving in unison with your arms, continuing the forward line of the stroke. When your arms pass your shoulders, your face should enter the water as your chest drops down and flops your arms forward. Your arms enter the water a moment after your head, as you achieve the "downhill" position.

Step 4: Continue into a third stroke. Stroke through to the rear, accelerating as you press against the water. As you finish the stroke quickly, allow your feet to snap down. Feel your upper body rise, and your face pop to the surface. Inhale looking down at the water directly in front of you. If you have maintained a stable head position, you should not be able to see the far end of the pool. Recover and feel your face

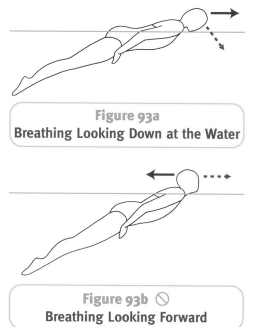

Figure 93a
Breathing Looking Down at the Water

Figure 93b ⃠
Breathing Looking Forward

submerge as your feet snap down again and you move into the "downhill" position.

Step 5: Perform a fourth stroke, accelerating through and allowing your feet to snap down as your finish your stroke. Feel your upper body rise. Inhale at your highest point, maintaining your head position. At the highest point, your chin should be just above the surface of the water, and you should be looking down at the water right in front of you. As you proceed into the recovery, drop your chest and face into the water. Notice that without changing your head position, you are again looking at the bottom of the pool.

Step 6: Practice more, achieving each breath within the line of your stroke. Maintain a stable head position throughout the stroke, so you are looking down at the bottom of the pool when your face is in the water, and down at the water in front of you when you are inhaling.

DRILL FEEDBACK CHART

Problem	Modification
My face doesn't pop out of the water.	Make sure you are finishing the stroke quickly, and that your feet are snapping down at the same time, giving you the lift you need to breathe. Also, make sure that your dolphin begins high in your body, and that you are not snapping your feet down as an independent action by over-bending at the knee.
I see the other end of the pool when I am inhaling.	This means you are raising your chin to breathe. Doing so compromises the straight spine line of the stroke. Instead, keep your chin down, so you will maintain a stronger position to start the next stroke.
My chin is much higher than the surface of the water when I am inhaling.	You might be pressing down on the water to achieve lift. Although you will be able to get your breath this way, it is very difficult to sustain high breathing, as you are spending a great deal of energy going up rather than forward.

Hammer and Nail

THE PURPOSE OF THIS DRILL
- Learning to breathe from the core
- Shifting to a "downhill" position after breathing
- Maintaining a stable head position

HOW TO DO THIS DRILL

Step 1: Push off the wall for the butterfly. Dolphin several times to establish rhythm, then start your arm stroke. Sweep through and accelerate to the rear. Finish fast as your feet snap down and feel your upper body rise. Inhale at the high point, looking down at the water. Recover, rolling your shoulders forward and dropping your chest down as your arms reach for the front. Feel your face return to the water and achieve the "downhill" position. Focus on what part of your face hits the water first.

Step 2: Do another stroke. After the inhale, as your arms and head move back to the starting position, freeze as your face hits the water. It should hit the water forehead first, rather than chin first. It should feel like your forehead hits like a hammer and the water is a nail.

Step 4: Do another stroke. As you accelerate to the rear and your upper body rises for the breath, focus on the arch of arms as they pass over the water. From the beginning to the end of the recovery, the forward movement of the arms is powered from the core, not the arms. The core action actually determines the line of the stroke. As you roll your shoulders forward, feel your head leave the high point of the stroke. As your hands pass your shoulders, and you drop your chest down into the water, the line of the stroke aims down and forward, bringing your face back to the water forehead first, and positioning your body "downhill" to begin the next stroke.

Step 5: Notice that without changing your head position at all, you rise from the water to breathe forehead first, and you also return to the water forehead first. Practice more, using your forehead as the

hammer to hit the nail that is the water. Do so with force, carrying the momentum of your recovery into the next stroke.

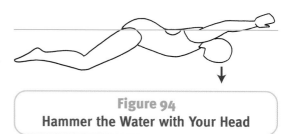

Figure 94
Hammer the Water with Your Head

DRILL FEEDBACK CHART

Problem	Modification
I hit the nail with my chin.	Make sure that you are maintaining a straight spine through to your neck throughout the entire breathing action. This means you are looking at the water during the inhale, not forward. Then, make sure that you are using your core to swing your arms around and forward during recovery, not just your arms. Roll your shoulders forward then drop your chest to change how your face enters the water.
When I hit the nail with my forehead my arms aim down.	Reach forward with your arms while your chest drops down. Doing so will allow you to keep moving forward while transitioning to the "downhill" position.
I don't feel momentum from the recovery.	Make sure your hands are relaxed, so they are not initiating the recovery. The motion should come from your core, in the middle of the arch of your two arms. Use your core to aim your body up and forward to breathe, and down and forward to return your face to the water, and to prepare for the next stroke.

LEVERAGE DRILLS

Leverage makes the butterfly work. Using it is necessary to perpetuate the forward momentum of the stroke for any length of time. While the whole body, from the hands through to the feet works as a lever, high hips are crucial to benefiting from its effects. Leverage in butterfly works between the upper body and the hips, and, between the hips and the feet. The goal of the following leverage drills for butterfly is to learn to position the body to make the most of the leverage at each stage of the stroke.

Advanced One-arm Butterfly 95

THE PURPOSE OF THIS DRILL
- Maintaining a high hip body position
- Feeling the hips as the center of the butterfly
- Using leverage in the butterfly

HOW TO DO THIS DRILL
Step 1: Push off the wall preparing to do the butterfly. Achieve a "downhill" float. Position your left arm at your side, while your right hand is extended in front of you. Perform a single butterfly stroke with your right arm, finishing quickly as your feet snap down, looking at the water in front of you as you inhale. Recover from the core, returning your face to the water and regaining your "downhill" position.

Step 2: Do another stroke with the same arm, focusing on your hips. When you are in the "downhill" position at the beginning of the stroke, your hips should be high. When you are in the inhale position, your hips should still be higher than your feet, though lower than your head. During recovery, when you are returning to the "downhill" position, and as your upper body travels down and forward into the water, your hips remain high.

Step 3: Continue your one-arm butterfly arm stroke, holding your hips high. Feel your upper body rise toward the end to the stroke. Feel it return to the "downhill" position at the end of the recovery. All the time your hips are high. Feel your feet snap down. Feel them rise. All the time your hips are high. Notice that your hips are the center of all the lever action in the stroke.

Figure 95
Advanced One-arm Fly

Step 4: Keep practicing the one-arm butterfly with your left arm at your side. Maintain high hips and feel the lever action in the stroke. Use it to achieve the "downhill" float. Use it to accelerate your stroke. Use it to inhale. Use it to recover. Use it to carry momentum into the next stroke.

Step 5: Continue to the far end of the pool. Switch arms and practice more.

DRILL FEEDBACK CHART

Problem	Modification
My hips sink when I am breathing.	This is the position when your upper body is a bit higher than your hips, but in relation to your feet, your hips should still be high. Maintain a firm core and make sure you are not lifting your upper body too high out of the water to breathe. Look down at the water and keep your chin close to the surface of the water.
My hips are not higher than my chest at the start of the stroke.	Drop your chest down as your arms reach forward. Carry the momentum of your recovery forward and down into your extended position. Also make sure you are not over-bending at the knee when you dolphin. Doing so will weaken the lever effect when you are transitioning to the "downhill" position.
When I dolphin my hips get lower.	What should actually be happening is that the hips are high to start, then they get even higher as the feet snap down. They return to the original position, which is lower than when the feet snap down, but they are still high in relation to the body.

No Kick Butterfly

96

THE PURPOSE OF THIS DRILL
* Achieving a dolphin without independent leg action
* Using leverage in the butterfly
* Powering the stroke from the core

HOW TO DO THIS DRILL

Step 1: Push off the wall for the butterfly. Achieve a straight spine, firm core and high hips. Lean into a "downhill" float and stretch your arms forward. Stroke through, and breathe when your upper body reaches its highest point. Recover using your core to propel your arms forward. Roll your shoulders forward and drop your chest down to return your face to the water.

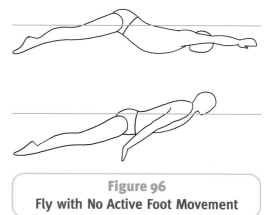

**Figure 96
Fly with No Active Foot Movement**

Step 2: Do another stroke, maintaining a high hip position, but purposely do not kick. From the "downhill" position, accelerate through the sweep of the arm stroke as your upper body rises. Breathe at the high point of the stroke. Notice that your feet snap down as you finish the arm stroke and breathe anyway.

Step 3: Recover, using your core to sweep your arms in a wide arch over the water. Return your face to the water as your chest drops, and your hands reach for the front. Notice that it is difficult to keep your feet from snapping down again after your chest drops into the water at the end of the recovery.

Step 4: In fact, the kick, or foot motion in butterfly is a result of the other actions of the stroke. Try it again. Holding a high hip position, but without actively kicking, sweep through to the back of the stroke. Feel your feet snap down as your upper body and head rise. Using your core, chest and shoulders, recover as your face returns to the water. Feel your feet snap down again as you reach forward.

Step 5: Continue doing the butterfly, producing a kick as a result of the actions of the rest of the stroke. Hold your core firm, and try to

make your feet snap down with force, only through the other movements of the stroke. Practice to the far end of the pool. Rest, then practice again.

DRILL FEEDBACK CHART

Problem	Modification
My feet don't snap down automatically.	Engage your core, and keep your spine straight. Without deliberately doing so, your lever will not work well, and your feet will not react to the other actions of the stroke.
When I don't kick, I can't breathe.	Maintain a high elbow position throughout the arm stroke, and finish the stroke with more speed. Press back on the water and avoid lifting it up at the finish. Doing so will pull you down into the water when it is time to breathe.
Without a kick, I am flat in the water.	Make sure your hips are high. Remember that they are the center of the stroke action. If they are not high, the leverage effect will be minimum.

97 No Pause Fly

THE PURPOSE OF THIS DRILL
- Establishing rhythm from the core
- Maintaining momentum and leverage
- Avoiding damaging pauses in the stroke

HOW TO DO THIS DRILL

Step 1: Push off the wall for the butterfly. Swim to the far end of the pool. Establish a rhythmic stroke, with evenly spaced kicks. If you aren't tired when you reach the wall, swim another length. As you reach the point where it is hard to maintain a rhythmic stroke, do a few more strokes, focusing on where in the stroke you lose your rhythm. Identify the point where your arms are when your rhythm breaks down.

Step 2: Notice that it happens after the arm entry, when your arms are extended. As you get tired, the extension at the "Y" position becomes a glide. When the arms come to a stop in front, rhythm is lost. When rhythm is lost, momentum and leverage are lost as well.

Step 3: Rest again. Now, push off the wall for the butterfly. Do only four strokes. Make each one a quick stroke. Focus on allowing no pause at the front of the stroke after your arms enter the water. Make a seamless transition from the recovery into the next stroke. Lay your hands on the surface of the water and grab hold of it. With your chest low in the water at this point, it should almost feel like you are reaching up with your hands.

Step 4: Rest and try it again. Do four quick strokes, grabbing hold of the water the instant your reach the "Y". With your chest low, anchor your hands in the water and vault your body forward over your hands. Actively involve your core in the transition to the next stroke.

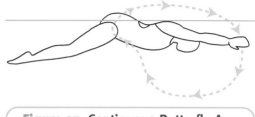

Figure 97 Continuous Butterfly Arm Motion – No Pause in Front

Step 5: Rest and then practice again. Achieve a chest-low position and reach into the "Y". Kick and feel the power of that kick move through your body. Use it to advance into your next stroke with absolutely no pause. Without pausing at the front of the stroke, you carry valuable momentum into the next stroke. Continue practicing No Pause butterfly, gradually increasing the number of strokes you do in a row.

DRILL FEEDBACK CHART

Problem	Modification
I don't feel like I am vaulting over my hands.	Make sure your elbows are straight and you achieve the "Y" position before starting the next stroke. Move your hands before your elbows.
I still have a pause at the front of my stroke.	Never stop your arm motion. Stretch forward then immediately sweep out and around. Actively space the down-beats of your dolphins to match the entry and the finish of your arm stroke.
I have a pause at the back of my stroke.	It could be that you are breathing as an independent action. If your head is rising too late, your arms will pause at the rear of the stroke. Let your breathing happen at the high point of the stroke.

COORDINATION DRILLS

A well-coordinated butterfly is a thing of beauty. The swimmer appears to move effortlessly through the water. Truly, a successful butterfly is less a matter of strength, and more a matter of a coordinated sequence of stroke actions. When the body position, dolphin action, arm stroke, recovery, breathing and leverage work together, the result is a butterfly that moves forward with rhythm, grace and power. The goal of the following coordination drills for butterfly is to practice the various actions of the butterfly in sequence so they benefit stroke as a whole, and improve the forward line of the stroke.

Chest Balance

THE PURPOSE OF THIS DRILL
- Benefiting from the "downhill" position
- Avoiding a flat butterfly
- Bringing momentum into the next stroke

HOW TO DO THIS DRILL
Step 1: Push off the wall preparing to do the butterfly. Achieve a straight spine, firm core and high hips. Sweep through and at the highest point in the stroke, take your breath. Recover, swinging your arms around and forward from the core. Notice that the breathing action is almost automatic. Perhaps because breathing is a matter of survival, it is a stroke action that we perfect early on.

Step 2: Take another stroke, and breathe when your upper body reaches its highest point. Freeze in that position. Notice that your forward motion quickly stops. While we

Figure 98 Balance on Your Chest

are good and practiced in achieving the breath, it is the part of the stroke after the breath that deserves attention in terms of maintaining the momentum and forward line of the stroke.

Step 3: Stroke again. Accelerate through, breathe, and recover. Notice that it takes deliberate action to get back to the "downhill" position. You have to actively to angle your upper body correctly, or you will end up flat, and without momentum for the next stroke. Try it again. Sweep through to the breathing position, then recover, actively regaining your "downhill" position, using your core and shoulders. Drop your chest down and lean "downhill". At this moment, your hips should be higher than your head. It should feel like you are balancing on your chest as you reach forward into the next stroke. Notice that by doing so you carry momentum with you into the next stroke.

Step 4: Take another stroke. Accelerate through, breathe, then deliberately use your core and shoulders during recovery to transition to the "downhill" position. Press your chest down and balance on it, feeling your body ride downhill. Stretch forward and begin the next stroke. Continue swimming butterfly for several strokes, focusing on achieving this chest balance point before beginning the next stroke. Rest, then practice again.

Step 5: Practice until balancing on your chest is as automatic as breathing.

DRILL FEEDBACK CHART

Problem	Modification
I don't feel like I am riding downhill when I balance on my chest.	Make sure your hips are high throughout the stroke. At the point when you are balancing on your chest, your hips should actually be higher than your head.
I end up very deep when I balance on my chest.	Make sure you are not riding downhill for too long. Maintain your forward momentum by balancing on your chest only for a moment as you move into your next stroke. Otherwise you will have to use your arm stroke to lift yourself to the surface rather than to move forward.
This means that at entry, my chest is lower than my hands.	Exactly. Just for a moment, balance on your chest as you achieve your maximum reach and best alignment, then move into the next stroke from a position of strength.

Coordination Checkpoint

THE PURPOSE OF THIS DRILL
* Coordinating the arms, legs and breathing
* Using momentum and leverage
* Achieving effortless breathing

HOW TO DO THIS DRILL
Step 1: Push off the wall for the butterfly. Sweep through the arm stroke, maintaining high, firm elbows. Sweep your hands closer together under your belly, then accelerate toward the rear. As you press quickly outward in a "J", feel your feet snap down and your face rise. Inhale. Notice three stroke actions happening simultaneously: the finish of the arm stroke, the inhale, and the down-beat of the second kick.

Step 2: Try it again. Sweep through the arm stroke, round off the finish as your feet snap down, and you achieve the high point in the stroke to inhale. Try it for several strokes in a row, focusing on the point when these actions happen at once.

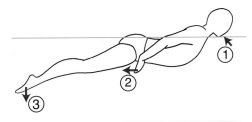

Figure 99 Coordination Checkpoint

Step 3: Notice that as these three actions happen at the same time, you can observe yourself surging forward through the water. Try it again. As your finish the stroke, and snap your feet down, look down at the water while inhaling. Notice your significant forward motion at this point.

Step 4: This is an excellent checkpoint for stroke coordination as you swim butterfly for any length of time. If the down-beat of your kick, the finish of your arm stroke, and your inhale do not happen together, the rhythm of the stroke suffers.

Step 5: Rest, then practice again, focusing on the coordination checkpoint every few strokes.

DRILL FEEDBACK CHART

Problem	Modification
I can't do this because I don't breathe every stroke.	Check your coordination on your breathing strokes.
My kick happens before my inhale.	Hold your kick until your arms are near the finish of the stroke so you can breathe at the natural high point of the stroke.
My inhale happens after my stroke finishes.	It is important to breathe with the end of the stroke to create a unified forward line in the stroke. Otherwise, your face will be moving back as your arms are moving forward, slowing you down.

100 Quiet Butterfly

THE PURPOSE OF THIS DRILL
- Achieving a clean entry
- Directing the stroke forward
- Swimming butterfly with the water, not against it

HOW TO DO THIS DRILL

Step 1: Stand in waist deep water. Bow forward until your chin rests on the surface of the water. Extend your arms forward aligned with your shoulders. Do four butterfly arm strokes and recoveries with your feet on the bottom of the pool, watching your point of entry in front.

Step 2: Look the splash that results as your hands enter. Notice the direction that the splash goes. This will tell you where your stroke is directed, and if you are swimming with the water or against it. Is the splash from your left arm crashing into the splash from your right arm? If so, you are directing your stroke side-ways, not forward. Is the splash from your hands going straight up? If you are directing your stroke down, not forward.

Step 3: Try it again. Stand in the water and bow forward. Do four complete strokes watching your entry. Aim each stroke forward at the end of recovery. At entry, lay your hands on the water, and slide them through the surface as you extend. Notice that the splash you make is minimal, and it is directed forward. Practice again, moving your arms with the water, not against it. Enter the water cleanly, displacing a minimum of water, and only in the forward direction.

Step 4: Now try it while swimming. Push off the wall for the butterfly. Do four stroke cycles focusing on directing each new stroke forward at entry. At the end of recovery, lay your hands quietly on the surface of the water. Slide them through the surface, fingertips first as you extend. Anchor your hands just below the surface of the water as your feet snap down. Sweep through and bring the momentum of your stroke and second dolphin into the recovery.

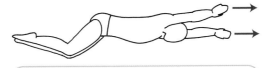

Step 5: At the end of recovery, reach forward to a "Y", not to the center. Slide your hands into the water without a sound, and extend and take hold of the water right under the surface, not more than a few inches deep. Direct all actions of the stroke to move you forward, quietly using the water, not fighting it.

Figure 100a
**Lay the Hands Forward
on the Surface of the Water**

Figure 100b ⊘
**Pressing Down
on the Surface of the Water**

DRILL FEEDBACK CHART

Problem	Modification
I have to slow my stroke down to enter the water without splashing.	At first you might have to slow down, but as you perfect your forward line you will be able to increase speed. Use the dolphin to provide momentum, then direct that momentum forward.
My hands go deep at entry.	Drop your chest down as you stretch your arms forward. Attempt to make no splash as you enter by laying your hands on the surface of the water.
My hands aim to the center at entry.	Try straightening your elbows as your reach forward in the recovery. Reach for the "Y" with your thumbs.

CONCLUSION

(5)

While there are enough great swimming drills out here to fill several volumes, I hope you have benefited from the 100 presented in this book. It has been my pleasure to witness each drill in this collection having a positive impact on the technique, economy and efficiency of swimmers I have coached. Just as every swimmer is unique, every swimmer has a favorite drill, one that has helped him or her feel and understand swimming better. It is my hope that this book becomes dog-eared and water-logged, as your poolside companion, along with your pull buoy and hand paddles, as you explore these drills, and that through focused practice, you find new favorites that lead you closer to the experience of more efficient swimming.

Meticulous editing provided by Bonnie Lucero. Support and patience provided by Vince Corbella.

The following swimmers pictured in this book were selected for their impeccable technique. In alphabetical order: Meredith Anderson, Jennifer Barra, Pam Bennett, Sarah Ebadi, Seth Goddard, Conny Bleul-Gohlke, Jonas Brodin, Chris Fish, Laura Howard, Katie Howard, Ellen Johns, Eric Johnson, Tami Kasamatsu, Bonnie Lucero, Siobhan Langlois, Blythe Lucero, Karen Matsuoka, Jessica Moll, Alvaro Pastor, Eric Rhodes, Dave Robert, Lynn Sun, Ian Umemoto, and, Nick Umemoto. Thank you for your great examples.

Catching the drills in action is a difficult task. It takes patience, expertise, and an understanding of swimming. In alphabetical order, the photographers responsible for the images in this book are: Vince Corbella, Sissela Danielson, Chaz Hubbard, Kurt Krueger, Blythe Lucero, Jonathan Newman, Roy Ramon Pelegrin, Lynn Sun, and Nick Umemoto. Thank you one and all.

And, thank you to Albany Pool and the City of Berkeley's King and West Campus pools for the water.

Illustrations by Blythe Lucero.

Cover photos: Imago Sportfotodienst;
© Jorge enrique Villalobos espinos/Hermera/Thinkstock;
© Fred_DL/iStockphoto/Thinkstock;
© Siarhei Pabylets/iStockphoto/Thinkstock

Cover design: Sabine Groten

Photos inside: Blythe Lucero

Page illustration number background:
© Nataliya Kostenyukova/Hemera/Thinkstock